WORLD OF WONDERS INSPIRING THE FUTURE

知の挑戦

Anthony Selli

John Barton

Ai Ogasawara

photographs by
©iStockphoto.com
Anthony Sellick
NASA and NSSDCA (National Space Science Data Center)
raneko via flickr

音声ファイルのダウンロード／ストリーミング

CD マーク表示がある箇所は、音声を弊社 HP より無料でダウンロード／ストリーミングすることができます。トップページのバナーをクリックし、書籍検索してください。書籍詳細ページに音声ダウンロードアイコンがございますのでそちらから自習用音声としてご活用ください。

https://www.seibido.co.jp

World of Wonders
Inspiring the Future

Copyright © 2016 by Anthony Sellick, John Barton, Ai Ogasawara

All rights reserved for Japan.
No part of this book may be reproduced in any form
without permission from Seibido Co., Ltd.

Preface

World of Wonders Inspiring the Future is the second in a series of books looking at a variety of important trends that are shaping the modern world. Each of the chapters examines a topic or issue that affects our lives, or which will change our lives in the future. We hope that you will find these topics interesting and thought-provoking. We also hope that they will be sufficiently stimulating to encourage you to learn more about these topics and issues.

The topics covered in the 20 essays range widely and are grouped into five distinct sections: the worlds of food, culture, science, business, and politics. The topics are drawn from a number of areas such as the world's favorite fruit (the banana), the history of spices, and the importance of sleep, through the impact of MOOCs (Massive Online Open Courses) and online shopping, to cyber warfare and international law. We hope that having read these essays, you will actively seek to develop your own views on the issues raised in this book, and that you will debate them vigorously.

As well as notes in Japanese following each essay, each chapter contains a pre-reading vocabulary exercise in the form of a short narrative related to the topic, and post-reading exercises are presented to test your comprehension of the essays. There is also a summary exercise for every chapter and a data analysis section for the odd-numbered chapters.

Finally, while we have tried to ensure that the material in this book is up-to-date, due to the fast-changing nature of some of the topics, it is inevitable that by the time the book is published, some things may have changed.

We sincerely hope you enjoy the book.

John Barton

CONTENTS

THE WORLD OF FOOD

Chapter 1 Flying Gold—Honey and Honey Bees
ミツバチと人の長い蜜月期(ハネムーン).. 1

Chapter 2 Worth Their Weight in Gold—The History of Spices
たかがスパイス、されどスパイス──歴史を変えた香辛料 6

Chapter 3 Superfood—The Incredible Banana
まさにスーパーフード！　驚異のフルーツ、バナナの秘密 11

Chapter 4 Golden Rice and Insect Burgers—The Future of Food
黄金米に虫バーガー？　食の未来予想図 16

THE WORLD OF CULTURE

Chapter 5 Glasses that Make You Smarter
—Wearable Technology and Augmented Reality
拡張する日常──ウェアラブル・デバイスとAR技術 21

Chapter 6 The World's Largest Schools
—The Increasing Popularity of MOOCs
オンラインでつながる「世界で一番大きな教室」...................................... 26

Chapter 7 Choices, Choices—How to Make Better Decisions
理性？　直感？　選択の極意とは 31

Chapter 8 There's No Such Thing as Trash
—How Innovators Turn Rubbish into a Resource
廃棄物を資源に変える革新者たち 36

THE WORLD OF SCIENCE

Chapter 9 Printing the Future—How 3D Printing Is Changing the World
3Dプリンターが変える世界と未来 41

Chapter 10 Tuesday's Child Is Full of Grace
—Does Your Birthday Affect Your Life?
生まれた日が運命を決める？　誕生日と統計的事実の相関 46

Chapter 11	A Good Night's Sleep—Why Do We Need to Sleep?
	ヒトと睡眠のメカニズム 51

Chapter 12	Space Age Gold Rush—Asteroid Mining
	宇宙時代のゴールドラッシュ——小惑星鉱業 56

THE WORLD OF BUSINESS

Chapter 13	Raising Money—The Crowdfunding Revolution
	10ドルの資金援助？　クラウドファンディングが変えるビジネス 61

Chapter 14	The Sweet Smell of Success—Using the Senses in Business
	成功の甘き香り——五感ビジネスの最前線 66

Chapter 15	Online Shopping—How It Has Changed the Way We Shop
	オンライン・ショッピングの"買い物革命" 71

Chapter 16	Tesla and the Electric Car —The New Age of Electric Automobiles
	新時代を開く電気自動車 76

THE WORLD OF POLITICS

Chapter 17	The Midas Touch—Can You Have Too Much Money?
	富の不平等がもたらすものは 81

Chapter 18	The Hidden Crime—Modern Slavery
	現在進行形の奴隷制の実態 86

Chapter 19	Someone Is Watching Me—Cyber-spies and Cyber-warfare
	サイバースパイ、サイバー戦争 91

Chapter 20	Everybody Wants to Rule the World —How Does International Law Work?
	高まる国際法の役割——真のグローバル社会へ 96

References 102

CHAPTER 1

Flying Gold
Honey and Honey Bees

GETTING READY

Choose the correct word or phrase from the list below to complete the story.

1. In 2012, beekeepers in Ribeauville in France had to destroy the honey their bees had _____.

2. This was because the hives did not _____ regular golden honey, but blue and green colored honey.

3. The farmers were worried and searched for _____ to explain the mysterious honey.

4. They discovered that large _____ candy from a local Mars factory were stored nearby.

5. The bees had been getting sugar from the colored candy instead of from local flowers and _____.

| amounts of | contain | crops | evidence | produced |

READING

1 Most people enjoy sweet foods. We even use words like sugar, sweetheart, sweetie, honey, and honeymoon in connection with love and romance. Of all the sweet foods that we eat, honey is probably the oldest. But have you ever thought about how we get honey, or about honey itself?

2 Honey is the only food eaten by humans that is produced by an insect. Honey is a food made by bees so that they have something to eat during the winter. To make honey, bees visit flowers, drink the nectar they make each day, and then return to the hive. Enzymes in the bees change the sugar in the nectar (sucrose), into the sugars that we like to eat (glucose and fructose). In the hive, the bees mix the nectar together and then let water evaporate from it. The result is honey, which is stored in a honeycomb made from beeswax. An average beehive contains between 20,000 and 40,000 worker bees, which collect the nectar. However, there is not much nectar in one flower, so for a beehive to make one kilogram of honey, the bees need to make about one million nectar-collecting trips. That means each worker bee in a hive must visit between 25 and 50 flowers for each kilogram of honey made by the hive. Each year, an average hive will produce around 20 kilograms of honey. No wonder we say someone who is very busy is a "busy bee."

The bees in an average hive like this will produce about 20 kilograms of honey every year.

3 In 2010, more than 1.5 million tons of honey, worth $1.2 billion, was consumed around the world. One quarter of all the world's honey comes from just one country, China. Africa and the European Union produce about 12 percent of the world's honey supply each, with the rest of the world producing the remaining 50 percent of the world's honey.

4 Honey is a special food. Because it contains a very high level of sugar and a very low level of water, bacteria and fungi cannot survive in it. As a result, honey is the only food that does not go bad. Furthermore, the different flowers visited by the honey bees all add different flavors to the honey, and honeys made by honey bees visiting just one kind of flower, such as heather or acacia, are very popular. Although honey is mostly made of different kinds of sugar, it also contains small amounts of vitamins and minerals including B vitamins, iron, magnesium, and zinc. As well as a food and a sweetener, honey is used in cooking and also to make an alcoholic drink called mead.

5 Honey is also used by doctors. Because bacteria and fungi cannot survive in honey, it is useful for treating infections that are resistant to antibiotics. There is also evidence that honey can help burns to heal more quickly. However, because honey sometimes contains botulinum spores, which can cause botulism, it shouldn't be given to children under one year old.

6 Honey is not the only product made by honey bees that humans use.

Beeswax is used to make candles, hand cream and other skin care products, cosmetics such as eye-liner and lipstick, chewing gum, medicine capsules, shoe polish, and surfboard wax. It is even used in surgery to stop bones from bleeding. Every year, around 10,000 tons of beeswax, worth $100 million, is used globally. However, the most important service provided to humans by honey bees is neither honey nor beeswax. It is fertilizing our crops. As the worker bees collect nectar, they also pick up pollen from the flowers. As they fly from flower to flower, the pollen is spread around, fertilizing the plants. With the exception of crops such as rice, wheat, corn, and barley which use the wind to spread their pollen, all of the crops we grow are fertilized by insects like bees. The value of the fertilization service provided by bees is estimated at $50 billion in Europe and more than $100 billion in Africa.

7 Without honey bees to fertilize our crops, we would struggle to feed ourselves, and our diets would have very little variety. Honey bees fertilize all of our fruits and nuts, most of our beans and vegetables, and many of our herbs and spices. Imagine living in a world without oranges, tomatoes, potatoes, grapes, chili peppers, coffee, or chocolate. As well as a boring and hungry world, we would lack clothes as well: cotton is also fertilized by honey bees. But this could be our future. As a result of pollution from pesticides used in agriculture, infection by the varroa mite, and climate change, honey bees have been dying in huge numbers in recent years. Unless we find ways to protect our honey bees soon, our 10,000 year honeymoon with honey may soon be over.

NOTES

Ribeauville「リボーヴィレ」フランス東部オー＝ラン県のコミューン(最小行政区)。ストラスブール南方75キロに位置し、ゴシック教会や古い街並みを残している。リボーヴィレ村では年間約1,000トンの蜂蜜を生産している。　**Mars**「マース」世界74カ国でペットケア、チョコレート、食品など6事業を展開し、年間売上330億ドルを計上するグローバル企業。1911年、米国ワシントン州で設立。M&M'S、Milky Way、スニッカーズなどのチョコレート菓子を販売している。　**hive**「ミツバチの巣」　**enzyme**「酵素、エンザイム」　**sucrose**「ショ糖、スクロース」　**glucose**「ブドウ糖、グルコース」人間の代謝作用の主たるエネルギー源　**fructose**「果糖、フルクトース (=fruit sugar)」果実や蜂蜜の中に存在する。　**honeycomb**「ミツバチの巣、ハチの巣、ハチの巣状のもの」直訳は「ミツバチのくし」で、ハチの巣状に正六角形または正六角柱が並ぶ構造をハニカム構造(honeycomb structure)と呼ぶ。工業的に応用されると軽くて丈夫な構造を実現するため、サッカーのゴールネットや飛行機の翼に利用されている。　**beeswax**「蜜蝋(みつろう)」ミツバチが巣作りのために分泌する蝋(ワックス)。　**European Union** = EU「欧州連合」　**fungi** fungusの複数形「菌、カビ」　**go bad**「腐る」　**heather**「ヘザー」各種ヒースの総称。ツツジ科の常緑低木で、小さな釣り鐘状の花をつける。　**zinc**「亜鉛」　**mead**「蜂蜜酒」ハチミツを原料とする醸造酒　**botulinum spores**「ボツリヌス菌の胞子」sporeは菌類・植物の胞子　**botulism**「ボツリヌス中毒」ボツリヌス菌による致命的な食中毒で、視覚障害や呼吸麻痺を起こす。　**fertilize**「受粉させる」　**varroa mite**「ミツバチヘギイタダニ、バロアダニ」ミツバチに害を与える寄生性のダニ

Questions for Understanding

Look at the following statements. Write T if the statement is True, and F if it is False. Write the number of the paragraph where you find the answer in the parenthesis.

1. _____ In order to make one kilo of honey, a bee must visit 40,000 flowers. (#   )

2. _____ According to the passage, China consumes 25 percent of the world's honey. (#   )

3. _____ According to the passage, honey can kill micro-organisms such as bacteria and fungi. (#   )

4. _____ The passage states that beeswax is the most valuable product humans obtain from bees. (#   )

5. _____ According to the passage, we rely on bees to help produce many of our food crops. (#   )

Summary

Fill each space with the best word from the list below.

| fertilize   sweetener   antibiotics   beeswax   doctors   heal |

Humans love sweet flavors, so it is no surprise that we love the taste of honey. However, honey is not only used as a 1)_____ in our cooking, it is also used by 2)_____ to 3)_____ burns because its high level of sugar kills bacteria as effectively as regular 4)_____. As well as honey, we also collect the 5)_____ that bees make, and use it in products ranging from candles to lipstick. Finally, bees 6)_____ our crops as they collect pollen, and this is the most valuable service they provide humanity.

Chapter 1 Flying Gold—Honey and Honey Bees

DATA ANALYSIS

Use the information in the passage to complete the table below.

Global Honey Production (2010)

	Proportion of global production	Weight (tons)	Value ($)
China			
Africa		187,500	
European Union	12.5%		
Rest of World			600 million
Total:	100%		

Chapter 2
Worth Their Weight in Gold
The History of Spices

GETTING READY

Choose the correct word or phrase from the list below to complete the story.

1. Curry is one of Britain's favorite foods. _____ one third of British people eat curry every week, and some famous dishes like chicken tikka masala were created in Britain.

2. If you _____ the history of curry, you soon find that the word "curry" mixes the French word "cuire" which means "to cook" and the Tamil word "kari" which is a kind of spicy soup.

3. Curry became popular worldwide after India became part of the British _____, and the first curry recipe in English was published in 1747.

4. However, this dish was very different from the traditional Tamil "kari." Chilies from South America had been brought to Asia in the 17th century, and it did not take long before Indian chefs used them to _____ their traditional dishes.

5. _____, modern curry is a truly international dish.

| investigate | flavor | empire | nearly | in other words |

READING

1 There is an English expression which is used to describe food that is very high quality. It is, "A meal fit for a king." Of course, royalty has always eaten much better food than regular people, but what does this really mean? Generally, ordinary people ate mostly vegetables, beans, and cereals. Fish would be eaten
5　much less often, and meat was a rare treat. Their food might be flavored with local herbs and salt, but the taste would often be very bland. In contrast, the

6

wealthiest people ate plenty of meat and fish with their vegetables, ate the freshest fruit, and had their meals flavored with honey, herbs, and exotic foreign spices. This is why we describe the very best meals as "fit for a king."

Shoppers buying spices in the Egyptian Bazaar in Istanbul, Turkey. This spice market has been operating since 1660.

2 Herbs and spices are often mentioned together, but they are not the same thing. Herbs are fresh or dried leaves used to flavor food. Basil, mint, and oregano are well-known examples of herbs. Spices are made from different parts of plants, but *not* the leaves. For example, pepper, ginger, and cinnamon are famous spices and are a fruit, a root, and the bark of a tree. For nearly 6,000 years, the trade in spices was one of the most important international businesses. Control of the spice trade made countries rich, caused wars, and encouraged voyages of discovery.

3 How is it possible that food flavorings could become so valuable? There are several reasons for this. Firstly, try to imagine what your food would be like if there was no sugar, pepper, curry, or any other spices in it. It would probably be somewhat boring. Secondly, as well as making food taste better, many spices have an antimicrobial effect. In other words, food cooked with spices stays good to eat for longer. In the days before refrigerators, this was very useful. Finally, almost all of the spices we use in our cooking come from Asia. For example, pepper comes from India, ginger from China, and cinnamon from Arabia, Sri Lanka, and China. Originally, these spices were traded along the Silk Road. Naturally, traders kept the source of these spices a secret in order to keep the prices high.

4 Until the end of the 18th century, the world's richest nations were China and India. The spice trade was one of the reasons that they were so wealthy. However, during the 15th century, the spice trade was disrupted by the Ottoman Empire. As a result, Europeans tried to find new ways to get their spices. Today, this era is known as the Age of Discovery, because it is the time when Europeans found ways to sail to India by going around Africa, discovered the Pacific Ocean, and also discovered North and South America. These discoveries enabled the Europeans to buy more spices at a much lower price. Unfortunately, the Europeans often decided to take over the countries and peoples they discovered. Soon England, France, Spain, Holland, and Portugal all had their own empires, which they controlled until the middle of the 20th century.

5 Today, spices are still an important commodity in international trade. The most valuable spice is saffron, which is part of a flower grown in West Asia, especially Iran. Saffron must be collected in the early morning and can only be collected for one or two weeks a year. To make one kilo of saffron, about 140,000 flowers must be collected. How valuable is saffron? In 1730, saffron was worth its weight in gold. In other words, one kilo of saffron and one kilo of gold had the same price. However, today one kilo of saffron is only worth about $10,000.

6 Saffron is used to flavor food, of course, but that is not its only use. Saffron also colors the food it flavors, and so it has also been used to dye cloth in some countries. It has also been used to make perfume. Today, scientists are investigating saffron as a possible treatment for some kinds of cancers and eye disorders. Saffron is not alone in having possible medical uses, however. Ginger is also being investigated as a cancer treatment, as is pepper, while cinnamon might help diabetics control their blood sugar levels. Hot spices like pepper could even help us to lose weight.

7 It is incredible to think that the spices we use in our food have been so strongly linked to important historical events like the discovery of the Americas by Europeans. Just as the spice trade led to the Age of Discovery, today scientists are discovering new things about spices and how they can help to keep us healthy. It is likely that spices will continue to be one of the most valuable commodities in the future.

NOTES

chicken tikka masala「チキンティッカマサラ」タンドリーチキン(スパイスに漬け込んだ鶏肉をかまどで炭火焼きにしたもの)を使った、マイルドな味わいのトマトベースのカレー。chicken tikkaは伝統的なインド料理で、タンドリーチキンの小片を意味する。masalaはスパイスをブレンドしたものを指す。ともにインドの伝統的な料理だが、チキンティッカマサラそのものは英国生まれで、現代の多文化的英国社会の象徴的料理。ブレア政権で外相を努めた故ロビン・クック氏は、チキンティッカマサラを「英国の真の国民食」(Britain's true national dish)と呼んだ。 **Tamil**「タミル族、タミル人の」インド南部やスリランカに住むタミル語を話す人々の総称。 **treat**「ごちそう、特別な楽しみ」 **bland**「うま味に欠ける、風味のない、刺激の少ない」 **basil**「バジル、バジリコ」シソ科の一年草。葉は芳香があり、香辛料として使われる。 **oregano**「オレガノ、ハナハッカ」シソ科の多年草。葉はほろ苦い爽やかな香りがし、香辛料として使われる。 **cinnamon**「シナモン、肉桂皮(ニッケイの樹皮)」香辛料や薬として利用される。 **bark of a tree**「樹皮」

Chapter 2　Worth Their Weight in Gold — The History of Spices

flavoring「調味料，香味料」　**antimicrobial**「抗菌性の」　**Ottoman Empire**「オスマン帝国（1299~1922)」トルコ族のオスマン一世を始祖とするイスラム帝国。欧州南東部・西アジア・北アフリカを支配した。　**Age of Discovery**「(the~) 大航海時代」15〜17世紀にかけて欧州諸国が航海・探検によって海外進出を行った時代。アフリカやアジアへの航路や、アメリカ大陸を発見したことから「(大)発見時代」とも呼ばれる。欧州による世界支配の契機となり、世界史に近代植民地体制の確立という転機をもたらした。　**take over**「奪う，(土地や地域を)占領する，(会社などを)乗っ取る，支配権を得る」　**saffron**「サフラン」アヤメ科の植物。その黄色の花の柱頭を乾燥させたものを香辛料や染料に用いる。　**diabetic**「糖尿病患者」

QUESTIONS FOR UNDERSTANDING

Check the best answer for each question.

1. Which of the following statements about spices is correct?
    a. ☐ Spices such as salt and pepper are used to flavor food.
    b. ☐ Spices are made from different kinds of leaves.
    c. ☐ Spices are made from plants, but not from their leaves.
    d. ☐ Ordinary people often used spices in their food.

2. Why were spices so valuable?
    a. ☐ Because they made food taste better.
    b. ☐ Because they stopped food from going bad.
    c. ☐ Because they had to be imported from foreign countries.
    d. ☐ All of the above.

3. What happened when the spice trade was disrupted?
    a. ☐ The Ottoman Empire was destroyed.
    b. ☐ China and India became the richest countries in the world.
    c. ☐ European countries started to build their own empires.
    d. ☐ Europeans created new spices.

4. Why is saffron so valuable?
    a. ☐ Because it is a perfume as well as a spice.
    b. ☐ Because it is very difficult to collect.
    c. ☐ Because it is a drug as well as a spice.
    d. ☐ Because saffron is made from gold.

Summary

Fill each space with the best word or phrase from the list below.

> bark   era   bland   Pacific Ocean   commodity   take over

Hungry? How about some tasty tree 1)_____? It seems strange that our love of spices has shaped history. In our modern 2)_____, we can eat an incredible range of food and flavors. However, food was often very 3)_____ for much of history. As a result, spices were an extremely valuable 4)_____ and when trade in them was disrupted, Europeans tried to 5)_____ the spice trade. In their quest for good food, they discovered the Americas and also crossed the 6)_____. Today, spices are just as important as ever, and some spices are even being studied as possible treatments for cancer and other diseases.

CHAPTER 3

Superfood
The Incredible Banana

GETTING READY

Choose the correct word or phrase from the list below to complete the story.

1. The banana is a _____ fruit enjoyed by people around the world.
2. However, while most people eat bananas, they can be used in many different ways, some more _____ than others.
3. In 2005, a British man entered a bookmaker's (a gambling shop) in London with a plastic bag _____ a banana.
4. He told the staff to give him money, but they knew that they were not _____, and just laughed.
5. Because the staff would not _____ him with any money, the man ran away. He was quickly stopped by the police, and went to jail for seven years.

| containing | nutritious | provide | (be) in danger | practical |

READING

1 The world's favorite fruit is the banana. Every year, more than 100 million tons of bananas are produced globally, which means bananas are the fourth most important crop after rice, wheat, and maize. Bananas are grown in more than 100 countries, but originally came from Asia. Today, more than 60 percent of the world's bananas are grown in Asia. India, China, and the Philippines are among the top banana-growing countries, producing more than one third of the world's bananas every year. Many scientists think that the banana was the first crop to be farmed, which means that people in Asia have been eating bananas for nearly 10,000 years. As a result, there are perhaps as many as 1,000 different kinds of banana grown around the world.

2 🎧 Bananas are tasty, of course, but why is the banana so popular? One reason that farmers like growing bananas is that they are easy to cultivate. More importantly, bananas are very nutritious. A 100g banana provides about 90 calories and is a good source of dietary fiber. In addition, bananas are a good source of B vitamins, and also contain vitamin C, and minerals such as iron, potassium, and manganese. Bananas can be eaten raw, baked, boiled, fried, and as dried chips. You can even make banana jam. As well as the fruit, banana flowers and part of the stem are often eaten as vegetables. Bananas are a popular snack, and many people like to eat a banana with milk for breakfast. Because bananas go well with milk, it should be no surprise that banana milkshakes are found on the menus of many fast-food restaurants. Mashed bananas, with or without milk, are also often used to feed babies as they switch from milk to solid food. Bananas are so nutritious that 500 million people in Africa and Asia eat them every day. For example, in Uganda, 75 percent of farmers grow some bananas, and they are part of nearly every meal.

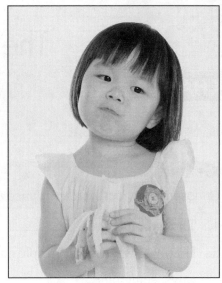

Bananas are a low-calorie snack that contain lots of vitamins and minerals. They taste good, too!

3 🎧 As well as snacks, milkshakes, and baby food, bananas can be used in many other ways. Because banana leaves are large and waterproof, in some countries in South and Southeast Asia, banana leaves are used for cooking food and as plates to serve food on. Banana leaves can even be used as umbrellas. The sap from the banana plant's stem can be turned into glue or ink. The fiber from banana plants has also been used to make rope, string, shopping bags, socks, and tea bags. In Japan, banana cloth has been used to make *bashōfu* clothes since the 13th century. The fiber from banana plants can also be used to make paper. In the Indian state of Gujarat and in the Philippines, banana paper is used to make bank notes. Does this mean that money actually grows on trees? Unfortunately not—the banana plant is not a tree. In fact, the banana is a kind of berry.

4 🎧24 Unlike most fruits, bananas do not have any seeds. This is because the banana plants we grow are mutants. There are more than 1,000 kinds of wild banana in Asia and they all contain lots of seeds. As a result, wild bananas have much less flesh for us to eat. Early human farmers chose mutant plants with fewer seeds and bred them together. Eventually, we produced plants with no seeds. That means that the banana plants we grow cannot breed and we have been growing clones of the original plants for thousands of years. While that means we have big, tasty fruit to eat, it also means that our banana plants have not changed genetically for a very long time. Unfortunately, plant diseases have changed a lot. For many years, the most popular kind of banana was the Gros Michel. You have probably never eaten one of these bananas because in the 1950s, a soil fungus called Panama disease rapidly destroyed the world's banana crop. Today, the most common commercial banana variety is the Cavendish banana. However, this variety is also under attack by several kinds of plant disease including the black Sigatoka fungus and a new form of Panama.

5 🎧25 Scientists are trying to create new varieties of banana that are resistant to these diseases, but it is very hard. Researchers in Honduras did develop a new variety of banana that was resistant to both diseases, but to do that they had to fertilize 30,000 banana plants by hand. From all that work, they only obtained a handful of fertile seeds. Genetic modification may be more practical, and scientists are now mapping the genome of the Cavendish banana and several varieties of wild banana to find genes that can resist disease.

6 🎧26 The banana is an amazingly versatile plant that feeds millions of people every day. However, because of the way humans have created the bananas we eat, they are in danger of disappearing from our diets. With luck, and hard work, modern science can rescue the banana so that we can continue eating them for the next 10,000 years.

NOTES

go to jail「刑務所に入る」　**maize**「トウモロコシ」maize flour トウモロコシ粉　**cultivate**「栽培する」　**dietary fiber**「食物繊維」　**potassium**「カリウム」　**manganese**「マンガン」　**Uganda**「ウガンダ」アフリカ東部の共和国。公式名は the Republic of Uganda（ウガンダ共和国）。**sap**「樹液」　***bashōfu***「芭蕉布」バショウ（芭蕉）はバショウ科の多年草。英語名をJapanese Bananaといい、沖縄や南九州に自生している。沖縄のバショウは大きく3種類あり、バナナを食べるための「実芭蕉（ミバショウ）」、繊維を取るための「糸芭蕉（イトバショウ）」、観賞用の「花芭蕉（ハナバショウ）」がある。イトバショウから採取された繊維で織られた布を芭蕉布という。沖縄の織物のなかで最も古く、13世紀ごろに織られるようになったと考えられている。**Gujarat**「グジャラート」インド西部の州　**bank note**「紙幣」　**mutant**「突然変異種」　**breed**「繁殖する」　**clone**「クローン，分枝系」1個の細胞または生物から無性生殖的につくられた、遺

伝的に同一の細胞または生物の集団。もとはギリシャ語で「小枝」を意味した。　**Gros Michel**「グロス・ミシェル」1900年代初めにジャマイカで発見されたバナナの一種。アメリカで瞬く間に人気となり、裕福な生産者が現れ「バナナ・ドリーム」という言葉を生み出した。パナマ病により、壊滅的な被害を受けた。　**fungus** Chapter 1のNotes（fungiの項）を参照　**Panama Disease**「パナマ病」これにかかるとバナナが枯れたり、黒ずむなどする。　**Cavendish**「キャベンディッシュ種」パナマ病に強いバナナの一種。日本で最も食べられている種類。　**the black Shigatoka**「ブラックシガトカ病，黒シガトカ病」シガトカ病はバナナ栽培における主要な病害で、黒シガトカ病はバナナの葉を黒く変色させ、光合成を阻害して収穫量を半減させる。　**resistant to ~**「～に抵抗力のある」　**Honduras**「ホンジュラス」中米の共和国。公式名は the Republic of Honduras（ホンジュラス共和国）。　**fertile seeds**「繁殖力のある種」　**genetic modification**「遺伝子組み換え」　**map** (v.)「（遺伝子情報を）解読する，マッピングする」　**genome**「ゲノム」ある生物の遺伝的特性全体を規定する遺伝情報の最小単位。構造としては染色体の一組に相当する。　**versatile**「用途の広い，使い道の多い」　**be in danger of ~**「～の危険がある」

QUESTIONS FOR UNDERSTANDING

Look at the following statements. Write T if the statement is True, and F if it is False. Write the number of the paragraph where you find the answer in the parenthesis.

1. _____ According to the passage, bananas were the fourth crop to be farmed, after rice, wheat, and maize.　　　　　　　　　　　　　　　(#　　)

2. _____ The passage informs us that bananas are grown by three quarters of Ugandan farmers.　　　　　　　　　　　　　　　(#　　)

3. _____ The passage describes how Japanese *bashōfu* cloth is used to make bank notes in India and the Philippines.　　　　　　　　　　　　　　　(#　　)

4. _____ According to the passage, the bananas that we like to eat are actually clones.　　　　　　　　　　　　　　　(#　　)

5. _____ Scientists are hoping to use genetic modification to create new varieties of banana.　　　　　　　　　　　　　　　(#　　)

SUMMARY

① 27

Fill each space with the best word or phrase from the list below.

soil　fungus　stem　breed　dietary fiber　glue

No other fruit is as important as the banana. The fruit's flesh provides us with energy, vitamins, minerals, and 1)_____, while the 2)_____ and leaves provide us with fibers and sap that can be used to make cloth, paper, and even 3)_____. However, bananas are under attack from different kinds of 4)_____ that live in the 5)_____. Unless we can find a way to 6)_____ new kinds of bananas, our favorite fruit may soon be a thing of the past.

Data Analysis

Use the information in the passage to complete the table below.

Part of banana plant	Uses	
Fruit	Food	Raw banana Baked banana Boiled banana Fried banana Dried banana chips _____ Mashed bananas / Baby food
	Drink	_____
_____	Food	
Stem	Food	
_____	Cooking _____ Umbrellas	
_____	Glue _____	
_____	Rope _____ Shopping bags Socks _____ Cloth Paper	

CHAPTER 4
Golden Rice and Insect Burgers
The Future of Food

GETTING READY

① 28

Choose the correct word or phrase from the list below to complete the story.

1. As _____ become wealthier, the food they eat also changes.
2. The _____ of these countries often includes more and more meat.
3. Meat _____ protein, which our bodies use to grow. As a result, as countries get richer, each new generation of children tends to be taller than the last.
4. For example, it is _____ that Japanese children today are 20cm taller than 100 years ago.
5. These children are also often healthier and more _____ disease because of the better quality food they eat.

| contains | resistant to | estimated | developing countries | cuisine |

READING

① 29~37

1 Consider these facts. Forty-two percent of the world's land surface is used for farming. About the same amount is desert, ice, or mountain. Today, one billion people do not have enough food to eat. By 2050, the global population will increase from 7 billion to between 9 and 12 billion people. Around 30 percent of
5　all the food that is produced is wasted.

2 Food security has shaped human history. It has started wars and caused civilizations to collapse. However, the food security crisis faced by humanity today can be solved. Let's look at the three main areas of food production: crops, fish, and meat.

3 Crops: Farmers face two big challenges. First, global warming could reduce the amount of farmland or reduce the ability of crops to grow. However, scientists developing genetically modified (GM) crops are finding ways to make crops more productive and more resistant to disease, drought, and flood. Some GM crops are being developed to meet other needs. For example, golden rice is a GM rice that contains vitamin A. Too little vitamin A causes blindness in 500,000 people and kills nearly 1.5 million every year.

How about a plate of tasty bugs? Is this the future of food for all of us?

4 Farmers also need to produce much more food on the same amount of land. Unfortunately, scientists cannot create new land for farming. Instead, scientists are moving farms to cities in special buildings called vertical farms. The first vertical farm opened in 2011 in New Buffalo in the United States, but they can now be found in many cities around the world, from New York to Kyoto. Vertical farms use much less power and fertilizer than traditional farms, and can produce almost double the amount of food. Some vertical farms use 98 percent less water than traditional farms. By 2050, the United Nations estimates that 85 percent of people will live in cities. Vertical farms will be essential in providing them with enough food.

5 Fish: Humans eat a lot of fish. The Food and Agriculture Organization (FAO) estimates that 75 percent of the world's fish stocks are either overexploited or at their maximum level of exploitation. This overfishing is changing the oceans. One change is a huge increase in the number of jellyfish because there are fewer fish to eat them. For example, the American warty comb jelly arrived in the Black Sea in 1982. By 1990, there were more than 900 million tons of them in the Black Sea. In some places, such as Namibia, there are now more jellyfish than fish. Unfortunately, while jellyfish are a traditional part of Chinese and Japanese cuisine, they are not very nutritious, having only 18 calories per 100 grams.

6 So what is the solution to overfishing? One response has been to create fish farms. Unfortunately, fish farms can produce a lot of pollution. In addition, they can be damaged by bad weather and other natural events. In 2007, 100,000 salmon on a fish farm in Ireland were killed by jellyfish. Is there a better way to farm fish? Once again, vertical farms may be the answer. There are already vertical fish farms in Hong Kong and Shanghai, and new farms will soon open in Singapore and South Korea.

7 **Meat:** People in developed countries eat an average of about 80kg of meat a year. In developing countries, the average is 33kg per person. However, one third of the crops we grow today are fed to animals to produce meat. How can we produce enough meat for everybody without destroying the world? One possibility is synthetic meat. In 2012, scientists in Holland cooked the first hamburger made with synthetic meat grown in a laboratory. This new technique holds much promise, but it will not be able to feed the world for a long time, if ever.

8 A more practical solution is to get the protein we need from insects. Insects can be found in the traditional cuisine of many cultures, from Mexico to Italy to Thailand to Japan. Around the world, more than two billion people eat insects every day. There are more than 1,900 kinds of insect that we can eat, and they are highly nutritious. Insects contain lots of vitamins, minerals and protein, but very little fat. They are also easy to farm. In fact, in Thailand alone there are already more than 20,000 insect farms. So why don't we all eat insects? In many developed countries, insects are generally thought of as pests that spread disease. As a result, the idea of eating them is often unpleasant. However, honey is a popular food, and some food colorings are made from insects. In these countries, it is likely that insects will slowly be added to our food as processed meat in burgers and sausages.

9 The menus of 2050 might look very different to the menus of today unless we change the way we think about food and farming. However, we could feed 10 billion people today if we reduced the amount of food we waste. That fact should make us think very hard about the lifestyle that we have become accustomed to.

NOTES

it is estimated that ~「～と見積もられている」　**food security**「食料安全保障」国連専門機関である国連食糧農業機関（Food and Agriculture Organization of the United Nations＝FAO）の公式ホームページによると、食料安全保障とは「全ての人が、常に活動的・健康的生活を営むために必要となる、必要十分で安全で栄養価に富み且つ食物の嗜好を満たす食料を得るための物理的、社会的、及び経済的アクセスが出来ることである」。食料の入手とその方法に関する国家レベルの論点。日本語で「食の安全」を意味する食品の安全性には"food safety"が用いられることが多

Chapter 4　Golden Rice and Insect Burgers —The Future of Food

い。 **genetically modified** (GM)「遺伝子組み換えの，遺伝子操作されている」 **be resistant to ~** Chapter 3 Notes参照　**vertical farm**「垂直農場」vertical farming「垂直農法・農業」は、高層ビルの階層や傾斜面を利用して農作物を垂直的に育てる方法。例えば、透明な壁から日光を取り入れ水耕栽培を行うことで農薬や化学肥料を使用しない有機作物を栽培するなど、安全な作物を都市で効率的に生産できる利点がある。　**Food and Agriculture Organization** (FAO)「国連食糧農業機関」経済・文化・教育等各分野において政府間協定によって設立された世界的専門機関のうち、国連総会の承認を受け国連経済社会理事会と連携関係協定を結んだ国連専門機関の一つ。1945年設立。本部はローマ（イタリア）で、196の加盟国（2つの準加盟国を含む）と欧州連合（EU）加盟国で構成される（2015年3月現在）。人々が健全で活発な生活を送るために十分な食料へのアクセスを確保し、全ての人々の食料安全保障を達成することを目的としている。　**overfishing**「（魚の）乱獲」　**comb jelly**「クシクラゲ」　**warty**「イボのある」　**Black Sea**「黒海」欧州とアジアの境にある内陸海　**Namibia**「ナミビア」アフリカ南西部の国。公式名はThe Republic of Namibia（ナミビア共和国）。　**cuisine**「料理」　**synthetic meat**「合成肉，人口食肉」　**if ever**「もしあったとしても極めてまれに」　**pest**「害虫」

QUESTIONS FOR UNDERSTANDING

Check the best answer for each question.

1. According to the passage, what is a vertical farm?

    a. ☐ A vertical farm is a farm that is on the side of a mountain.

    b. ☐ A vertical farm is a farm that is underground.

    c. ☐ A vertical farm is a farm that is in a city building.

    d. ☐ A vertical farm is a farm that floats on the ocean.

2. What is a result of overfishing described in the passage?

    a. ☐ Chinese and Japanese cuisine has changed.

    b. ☐ Fish from the Black Sea have moved to Namibia.

    c. ☐ People have started to eat jellyfish instead of fish.

    d. ☐ Jellyfish have replaced fish in many places.

3. Why do people from some countries think eating insects is disgusting?

    a. ☐ Because insects cause trouble and spread diseases.

    b. ☐ Because insects are very nutritious.

    c. ☐ Because insects do not contain much fat.

    d. ☐ Because only people from four countries eat insects.

4. According to the passage, why should we "think very hard about the lifestyle that we have become accustomed to"?
   a. ☐ Because the food we will eat in the future will be different to the food we eat today.
   b. ☐ Because there will be nearly 10 billion people living in the world in the future.
   c. ☐ Because there is more than enough food for everybody, but we waste too much.
   d. ☐ Because it is important to have a healthy diet as we get older.

SUMMARY

Fill each space with the best word or phrase from the list below.

| desert | (be) worried about | collapse | tend to |
| exploit | become accustomed to | | |

Many scientists and politicians 1)_____ food security. As countries get richer their citizens 2)_____ eat more meat. The problem with this is that we already 3)_____ nearly all the land that is suitable for farming and are overfishing the seas. The result is that some farms are turning into 4)_____, and the seas are filling with jellyfish instead of the fish we like to eat. If we do not want our food supply to 5)_____, we must find new ways to farm, and new foods to eat. It may be that future generations will need to 6)_____ plates of insects and jellyfish instead of salmon and steak.

CHAPTER 5

Glasses that Make You Smarter
Wearable Technology and Augmented Reality

Getting Ready

Choose the correct word from the list below to complete the story.

1. The Pebble watch is an example of _____ technology and was one of the first smart watches.

2. The company _____ the product in 2013 after raising start-up money of over $10 million on Kickstarter.

3. You can wear the _____ on your wrist for maximum convenience.

4. The watch can _____ the time, incoming e-mails, and fitness data.

5. The company has produced several new models and has quickly _____ a lot of happy customers.

| gained | launched | device | display | wearable |

Reading

1 The availability of wearable technology has grown rapidly in recent years as companies take advantage of the possibilities offered by GPS, widespread wireless Internet, smartphones, and smartphone applications. Consumers can now choose from a wide range of wrist bands, glasses, sleep sensors, ultra-violet sensing hairbands, heart-monitoring armbands, brainwave monitors, and even bras. Most of these devices function by communicating with your smartphone, which provides computing power and Internet access. By using these devices, we are able to more deeply understand our own bodies, our own lives, and our own environment. It is perhaps true that so far, this type of technology has

21

appealed to certain "geeky" markets – the fitness fanatic or the health freak. This seems set to change, however, as the biggest brands start producing wearable technology. When Apple launched its Apple Watch in 2015 it announced that "Apple Watch represents a new chapter in the relationship people have with technology." According to Apple, the Apple Watch is its most personal product, because it is the first that it has designed to be worn. In time, it seems likely that everything we now do with a smartphone will be possible using a single device that we wear.

The information that wearable technology like this smartband can provide could revolutionize our health and how we live our lives.

2 There are many different kinds of wearable technology. For example, Google manufactured a special pair of glasses known as Google Glass. The lenses could display your e-mail, directions to a place you wanted to go, running data such as your speed and average time, and show you which music track you were listening to. It could even act as a range finder on a golf course and display how far you had to the hole. Google Glass was experimental, but in the future Google plans to sell a product with even better capabilities.

3 Another piece of wearable technology is the Fitbit. Fitbit was founded on the idea that exercise is not just something you do at the gym but something you can do all the time. Fitbit claims that, "Every moment matters and every bit makes a big impact." You clip your Fitbit either to your clothing or wear it on your wrist. The data you generate from your daily activity then syncs wirelessly with your smartphone and an Internet website which records your achievements, helps you set goals, and helps you reach your targets whether they be weight loss or preparing for a particular sporting event.

4 Undoubtedly, there are many benefits to be gained from these devices. Their small size and portability makes them very convenient. Also, by capturing various data, it is possible to measure your progress towards your wellness and fitness goals. A device like Fitbit can track your activity level, exercise, sleep, food, and weight. Most fitness applications also have a social element meaning

Chapter 5   *Glasses that Make You Smarter* — *Wearable Technology and Augmented Reality*

that you can share your achievements with your friends or invite them to join you for a bike ride. This social connectivity also helps to keep motivation high.

5   Some sports teams also use these devices to improve the performance of their athletes. For example, the Dallas Mavericks, an American professional basketball team, uses a wrist band called "Readiband" to monitor the players' sleep. They argue that the better you sleep, the better you play because of improved reaction times. Some companies such as eBay, BP, and Coca Cola are also asking their employees to wear fitness tracking devices in order to encourage increased health among employees. Employees that agree to do this receive discounts on their health insurance payments. Other companies such as Bank of America have used wearable technology to study the movements of their call-center employees in order to make changes that improve productivity.

6   Inevitably, there will be some drawbacks to wearable technology. Employers may use these devices to uncover information that the employee would prefer to keep private, such as where they go during and after work, or their stress levels. In the future, you may have to provide a bio-CV that will include your health measurements, stress level, fitness level, how well you sleep, and more. Another concern is the fact that many kinds of wearable technology such as Fitbit post information online. At the moment, it is not clear who owns this data or how it will be used. In particular, it is not clear if wearable technology companies have the right to sell the data you share with them.

7   For many, wearable technology promises a future where people are fitter and more in control of their health. Companies hope that it will make their employees more productive, engaged, and effective. Sports coaches hope it will help their players to win more games and become more successful. Wearable technology has come a long way in a very short time. It seems certain that in the near future, we will all be monitoring some part of our lives with a wearable device.

NOTES

wearable technology「ウェアラブル・テクノロジー」ウェアラブル・デバイスの開発や製品化に関連する技術の総称。その技術によって生み出された製品（ウェアラブル・デバイス）の総称としても用いられる。 **wearable device**「ウェアラブル・デバイス，ウェアラブル端末」腕時計のように腕に巻く、眼鏡のようにかけるなど、身体に装着して利用できるコンピューター端末（デバイス）の総称。Apple Watch やGoogle Glassがウェアラブル・デバイスの代表例。 **augmented reality (AR)**「拡張現実」人が知覚する現実世界の情報に、デジタル合成などで作成された情報を付加し、人の現実認識を強化する技術のこと。例えば、目の前の風景にARのアプリを実装したスマートフォンのカメラをかざして見た場合、スマートフォンの画面上にその風景の中に映る建物の名前などの情報が表示されることが可能となる。このように、現実の環境をコンピューターによって「拡張」する技術。拡張されて知覚される環境そのものを指す場合もある。

Pebble watch「ペブルウォッチ」スマートウォッチや腕時計型端末と呼ばれ、腕時計のように手首に巻きつけて装着するウェアラブル・デバイス。時計として使えるほか、無線通信によってスマートフォンと連携して使用できる。米国のクラウドファンディングのサイトKickstarterで多額の出資を集め注目される。 **Kickstarter**「キックスターター」米国で2009年から開始された"クリエイティブな"プロジェクトにクラウドファンディングで資金を調達するためのサービス（インターネットサイト）。（クラウドファンディングについては Chapter 13 を参照）インターネットを通じて不特定多数の人から資金を集めるクラウドファンディングの中でも最も知名度が高く規模も大きい。プロジェクトの考案者（creator）はキックスターターでプロジェクトを発表し、賛同者・協力者となる一般個人ユーザー（backer）から広く資金を集め、プロジェクトの実現やアイデアの商品化を目指す。プロジェクトは映画、ゲーム、音楽、デザイン、テクノロジーなどに関連するもので、2009年のサービス開始以来、920万人が9万件のプロジェクトに19億ドル以上を投資している（2015年8月現在）。 **incoming e-mail**「受信Eメール」←→outgoing e-mail **take advantage of** ~「～をうまく利用する、～を活用する」 **GPS**=global positioning system「全地球測位システム」米国が管理する24個のGPS衛星（人工衛星）からの電波を受信し、地球上のどこにいても高精度で位置を計測できるシステム。最近ではスマートフォンやノートパソコン、防犯装置などに搭載され、応用範囲が広がっている。 **application**「アプリケーション、アプリ」アプリケーション・ソフトウェア（application software）の略称。英語では略語としてapp（App）が用いられる。日本では一般にソフトウェアあるいはソフトと呼ばれていたが、スマートフォンiPhoneの普及とともに「アプリ」と呼ぶことが一般的となった。 **geeky**「オタクの」 **fitness fanatic**「フィットネス狂」fanaticは「狂信者、マニア」の意 **health freak**「健康マニア」freakは「熱狂的愛好家、ファン、マニア」の意 **range finder**「レンジ・ファインダー、光学視差式距離計」 **Fitbit** 米 Fitbit社の製品で、身に着けることでその人の健康状態を記録するウェアラブル・デバイス。歩数、移動距離、消費カロリー、睡眠状態などを記録する。万歩計のような形や、リストバンド様の製品、腕時計型の製品もある。 **sync**=synchronize「同期する、同期させる」 **Dallas Mavericks**「ダラス・マーベリックス」米国テキサス州ダラスを本拠地とするNBA（全米プロバスケットボール協会）のチーム。 **Readiband** カナダのFatigue Science社が開発した腕時計型のウェアラブル・デバイス。社名が示す通り、疲労度の測定と、疲労によるリスクの軽減やパフォーマンスの向上を目的としている。Readibandを装着して数週間過ごすと、その人の睡眠時間帯や睡眠の量、活動時間を記録し、行動パターンを分析、疲労の管理や生産性の向上につなげることが可能となる。 **eBay** 米国の企業。世界規模のインターネットオークションサイトeBayを運営。 **BP** 英国の総合エネルギー企業。2001年にBritish PetroleumからBPに社名を変更した。 **bio-CV** CV=Curriculum Vitae「履歴書」 **post**「（インターネット上に情報を）掲載する、投稿する」 **come a long way**「大きな発展（進歩・成長）を遂げる」

QUESTIONS FOR UNDERSTANDING

Look at the following statements. Write T if the statement is True, and F if it is False. Write the number of the paragraph where you find the answer in the parenthesis.

1. _____ According to the passage, most wearable devices connect directly to the Internet. (#)

2. _____ It is likely that wearable devices will replace smartphones in the near future. (#)

3. _____ Fitbit is a device that is aimed mainly at professional athletes and sportspeople. (#)

4. _____ Companies such as Coca-Cola require their employees to wear a device while they are at work. (#)

Chapter 5 *Glasses that Make You Smarter — Wearable Technology and Augmented Reality*

5. _____ In the future, companies may require that you disclose information about your health and fitness levels before offering you a job.

(#   )

SUMMARY

Fill each space with the best word from the list below.

benefits   availability   inevitably   achievements   productive   monitor

The 1)_____ of smartphones and the Internet has led to a great deal of interest in wearable technology. Many devices such as Fitbit focus on fitness and health 2)_____. Devices such as these can provide measurement and motivation, and help people to make many satisfying 3)_____. Sports teams and companies also like the idea of wearable technology as they can lead to improvements in performance and can make people more 4)_____. 5)_____, there is a darker side to this technology. Companies may use it to 6)_____ the private lives of their employees, for example. Despite these concerns, it seems that wearable technology is going to become an increasing part of our lives.

DATA ANALYSIS

Use the information in the passage to complete the table below.

Name of Technology	Where you wear it	What it can do
Google Glass		Displays e-mails, directions, golf course information
	On your wrist	In time, will have the functionality of a smartphone.
Fitbit		Measures sleep, exercise, weight
		Measures sleep patterns for sports players such as the Dallas Mavericks.

CHAPTER 6

The World's Largest Schools
The Increasing Popularity of MOOCs

GETTING READY

Choose the correct word or phrase from the list below to complete the story.

1. Today, many different kinds of distance learning are _____. But how did distance learning start?

2. The first distance learning courses were begun by Isaac Pitman in England in the 1840s to teach shorthand, and _____ the new postal service.

3. Lessons were sent on postcards, and students also completed their _____ on postcards and sent them back to the teacher so that they could be checked.

4. This process of students and teachers giving each other feedback is what made the system successful, and the same _____ can be found in nearly all distance learning courses today.

5. While distance learning courses first began teaching skills like shorthand, it is now common for people to _____ university degrees by distance learning.

| obtain | principle | took advantage of | available | assignments |

READING

1 MOOC stands for Massive Open Online Course. They are courses of study that are taught online and many are free. This means that if you have an Internet connection and a computer, you can participate. MOOCs are very wide ranging. You can do anything from learning how to play the guitar to advanced
5 computer programming.

2 A typical MOOC is composed of a set of videos and readings presented

Chapter 6 The World's Largest Schools — The Increasing Popularity of MOOCs

by the teacher and then a series of quizzes or assignments that you have to complete in order to pass the course. As with a traditional classroom setting, you are able to interact with the teacher and all the other students but you have to use electronic means such as e-mail and the online forums that are usually featured as part of the course. In addition, many students set up virtual study groups and sometimes, if they are in the same city or part of the world, real-life study groups.

The interconnected world means that a student studying alone may actually be part of a class of thousands.

3 There are now thousands of these online courses available from a variety of providers including Coursera, FutureLearn, Canvas, EdX, and JMOOC. In addition, several universities offer MOOCs directly from their own websites, such as Harvard University and Massachusetts Institute of Technology.

4 In July 2015, Coursera, which was launched in the first half of 2012 and is one of the first MOOC providers, had over 14 million people participating in its courses worldwide. It ran 1,069 courses from 122 educational partners around the world including Stanford, Yale, Tokyo, and Shanghai Universities.

5 Distance or remote learning has existed for a long time, but MOOCs have changed the industry dramatically. One of the first classes taught in this way was by Andrew Ng at Stanford University on the topic of machine learning. The normal enrollment in the class was 400. When it was offered online 100,000 people signed up. It is the possibility for so many people from all around the world to study together that makes MOOCs special. Unlike some kinds of online studying, MOOCs offer a truly interactive experience. Some courses, for example those with clear right or wrong answers, work well with immediate feedback quizzes. Some subjects, such as philosophy and politics, however, need something a little different as answers to complex questions are not clear-cut. Naturally, a professor cannot check 100,000 students' answers, so many MOOCs use peer assessments instead. Peer assessments are when students mark the assignments submitted by other students. Research has found that scores awarded by students and the scores awarded by professors tend to correlate

quite closely. This means that even very large student enrollments are able to get their assignments marked and obtain meaningful feedback.

6 MOOCs are very good for students in several ways. Courses are often free so there is no financial barrier to learning. According to some reports, the cost of higher education in the United States has risen by 559 percent since 1985. These free courses open doors of opportunity to those who otherwise would not have the chance to study university-level courses. These online courses can also benefit citizens from poorer countries that traditionally do not have access to first-rate education. MOOCs also open up ongoing educational opportunities for those in more developed societies whose commitments or financial resources do not allow them to attend courses at higher education institutions.

7 MOOCs are also good for teachers. Instead of 30 people in your physical classroom, you may be able to reach 30,000 or more via a MOOC without having to grade every one of them. Teachers can also view all the data submitted by the many students and can target common errors and then fix them. MOOCs are also good for universities. They can get increased exposure and positive public relations benefits from taking part. Many courses offer different levels of certification for a small fee, with some even providing regular university credit, which allows MOOCs to become an additional source of revenue for the universities that create them.

8 Today, more and more people are accessing education and pursuing life-long learning goals through MOOCs. Online education is creating an environment where the playing field is a lot flatter—the world of education has been democratized through the availability of technology. Coursera was founded on the principle that education is a human right. MOOC providers like Coursera and others allow anyone with an Internet connection and a computer to take advantage of this amazing development in education. As Plutarch said, "the mind is not a vessel that needs filling, but wood that needs igniting." Time will tell how many minds are ignited by MOOCs.

NOTES

Isaac Pitman「アイザック・ピットマン(1813-1897)」英国の教育家。英語の発音に忠実なピットマン式速記を発案。これは最も普及した速記方式で、世界各国の速記に影響を与えた。　**shorthand**「速記，速記法」　**take advantage of** ~ Chapter 5のNotesを参照　**MOOC**=Massive Open Online Course「大規模公開オンライン講座，ムーク」複数形ではMOOCs =「ムークス」と呼ばれる。　**stand for**「（略語などが）~を表す」　**be composed of** ~「~から成り立つ」　**Coursera**「コーセラ」米スタンフォード大学のDaphne Koller（ダフニー・コーラー）教授およびAndrew Ng（アンドリュー・ネグ）准教授によって2011年秋に設立されたソーシャルベンチャー

Chapter 6　The World's Largest Schools — The Increasing Popularity of MOOCs

企業が提供するオンライン講座。　**FutureLearn**　英国のOpen Universityが2013年9月から講座を開始したMOOCsの英国最初のプラットフォーム。英国内外の大学、ブリティッシュ・カウンシル（英国の公的な国際文化交流機関）、大英博物館、大英図書館などが連携している。Open University（オープン・ユニバーシティー）は1969年に設立された英国国立大学。世界で初めて遠隔教育を中心とした高等教育に成功した。日本の放送大学のモデルである。**Canvas**　米国ユタ州の教育情報企業Instructure社（2008年～）が2011年から提供する学習管理システム（Learning Management System: LMS）。LMSはeラーニングを実施するために必要なシステムで、インターネットを通じてeラーニングを配信するプラットフォームのこと。学習教材の配信や成績などを管理する。　**EdX**　「エデックス」マサチューセッツ工科大学（MIT）とハーバード大学を中心として生まれたMOOCのプラットフォーム。2012年秋から開始した。カリフォルニア大学バークリー校、北京大学、京都大学などが参加している。　**JMOOC** = Japan MOOC「ジェイムーク」日本のMOOC、の意。日本版MOOCの普及を目指し、2013年に一般社団法人「日本オープンオンライン教育推進協議会」（略称JMOOC）が設立された。2014年4月に3講座が開講し、順次講座が開講されている。　**Andrew Ng**「アンドリュー・ネグ」スタンフォード大学の准教授で、Courseraの共同設立者の一人。「機械学習」（machine learning）「データベース」「人工知能」などのオンライン授業を2011年10月期から無料で配信。　**enrollment**「（受講）登録者数」　**sign up**「受講・参加登録をする」　**first-rate**「一流の，最上の」　**via**「～経由で」　**public relations**「広報（活動），PR」

QUESTIONS FOR UNDERSTANDING

Check the best answer for each question.

1. According to the passage, which of the following is correct about MOOCs?

    a. ☐ MOOCs and the traditional classroom setting are the same.

    b. ☐ Students and teachers of MOOCs communicate electronically.

    c. ☐ It is important for MOOC students to set up virtual study groups.

    d. ☐ It is important for MOOC students to set up real-life study groups.

2. According to the passage, why is peer marking so important for MOOCs?

    a. ☐ Because peer marking is accurate and allows many students to learn together.

    b. ☐ Because peer marking is inaccurate and allows many students to learn together.

    c. ☐ Because peer marking works best when there are no clear-cut answers.

    d. ☐ Because peer marking works best when there are clear right or wrong answers.

3. What two reasons does the passage give for why universities make MOOCs?
   a. ☐ The universities can make extra money.
   b. ☐ The universities can find common errors.
   c. ☐ The universities can become more widely known.
   d. ☐ The universities can view all of the students' data.

4. What do you think the expression "the world of education has been democratized through the availability of technology" means?
   a. ☐ People can use the Internet to vote for their favorite courses and teachers.
   b. ☐ People can use the Internet to study no matter who they are.
   c. ☐ People can use the Internet to learn about democracy.
   d. ☐ People can only use the Internet in democratic countries.

Summary

Fill each space with the best word or phrase from the list below.

revenue   sign up   interact with   certification   exposure   participate

MOOCs are a new kind of distance learning. Students can 1)_____ in courses offered by the best universities in the world for free. Although there may be as many as 100,000 students taking a course at the same time, MOOCs can still feel like a small classroom because students can 2)_____ each other in online forums. Many MOOCs offer some kind of 3)_____, either for free or for a small charge, to students who successfully complete them. Universities benefit from providing MOOCs by earning 4)_____ from the sales of certificates. They also benefit from the 5)_____ that MOOCs give them, because more students 6)_____ with them to study.

CHAPTER 7

Choices, Choices
How to Make Better Decisions

GETTING READY

① 58

Choose the correct word or phrase from the list below to complete the story.

1. This is a chapter about how to choose well, so let's begin by _____.
2. You _____ two doors. Behind one door is your lover. Behind the other door is a hungry monster. You must open one door.
3. There are also two _____ notes, one on each door. The note on door A says, "Behind this door is your lover, and behind the other is the monster." The note on door B says, "Behind one of these doors is your lover, and behind one of these doors is the monster."
4. You only _____ one piece of information to solve this puzzle. That information is that one of the notes is true, and the other note is false.
5. Can you work out which door to open, or will you go with your _____ and guess?

| nearly identical   (be) faced with   require   making a decision   gut feeling |

READING

① 59~65

1 CD 59 We are all constantly faced with decisions. Decisions range from the simple, such as which shirt to wear in the morning to the much more complex and important decisions such as whether to get married, make an investment, or which car to buy. Some people such as pilots or members of the military are faced with making decisions in life-or-death situations. So how can we make better decisions? The simple answer is by beginning to understand more fully how the brain works and knowing which parts of the brain to use in different situations.

2 CD 60 It was Plato who originally suggested that the mind was separated into

31

two parts: a rational, logical part and an emotional part. He argued that when making decisions we should try to use the rational part of the mind and keep our emotions under control. He thought that emotions were a negative influence when making decisions. Despite being accepted for thousands of years, recent work by scientists has come to some very different conclusions that require us to rethink our Platonic decision-making model.

How can we make sure that the choices we make are the best ones?

3 By using brain scanning technology, scientists have discovered that we often make decisions using both the parts of the brain that are associated with emotions *and* the parts involved with rational thought. Much of the key work in this area has been done by Wolfram Schultz, a neuroscientist at Cambridge University. What he has discovered is that some of our decision-making processes and experiences can become encoded as an emotional "gut feeling." Take the example of choosing clothes that coordinate, some clothes just feel "right" together while other combinations just feel "wrong." This is the effect of our experiences being encoded as an emotional response.

4 Why might this "gut feeling" be useful? Take the example of a radar officer on board an aircraft carrier during the First Gulf War in 1991. One day he saw a signal on the radar screen that could have been an enemy missile or a friendly plane. Acting on a "gut feeling," he decided to shoot down the incoming object. It turned out to be an enemy missile. His actions saved hundreds of lives, but the operator himself did not understand why his decision was correct until it was studied by a neuroscientist. What the neuroscientist discovered was that, because of his extensive training, the radar operator's brain had learnt to have an emotional response to certain patterns on the radar screen. As a result, the radar operator had felt scared when he saw the unusual signal on the radar screen and so decided to shoot down the object. If he had tried to decide if the object was a missile or a friendly plane using rational thought, he would have been overwhelmed by the amount of information and would probably have taken too long to make a decision. In other words, an emotional "gut feeling" is a much faster way to make a decision than rational thought.

5 Work by Dutch scientist Ap Dijksterhuis showed how understanding the two different ways we think can help us to make better decisions. In his experiment, people were asked to imagine that they were going to buy a new car. Some people were given four pieces of information about the car while others were given 12 pieces of information. What he discovered was that the more information people had, the harder they found it to choose which car to buy. What this means is that when people are faced with a simple decision, it is better to rationally think through the options before deciding, but when the decision is more complex we tend to become confused by the different options and it is better to rely on our emotions when deciding.

6 And this, in fact, does seem to be how we make many of our decisions. If we want to choose which of three nearly identical frying pans we should buy, most of us would probably choose the cheapest one—a rational decision. On the other hand, when buying a new car, we will often choose the one that "suits us" and then use the information about the car to confirm (or reject) our original decision.

7 This is a very simple introduction to the science of decision-making, and inevitably there are many other elements related to good decision-making. If there is one useful thing to learn about decision-making, it is that we should think about thinking. Whenever we make a decision, we should be aware of the kind of decision it is and the thought processes it requires. If you can begin to understand these processes then you will set yourself up for much better decision-making in the future.

NOTES

work out「（問題などを）苦労して解く・解決する，（方法などを）考え出す」 **go with one's gut feeling**「勘で決める，勘に従う，直感にまかせる」 **identical**「同一の，全く同じ」 **range from ~ to ...**「〜から…まで及ぶ」 **Plato**「プラトン」古代ギリシャの哲学者。ソクラテスの弟子。 **Wolfram Schultz**「ウォルフラム・シュルツ」英国の神経学者 **encode**「（情報などを）符号化・コード化する」 **on board**「（船・飛行機などに）乗って」 **aircraft carrier**「航空母艦」 **the First Gulf War**「第一次湾岸戦争」1990年8月のイラクによるクウェート侵攻をきっかけに国連が多国籍軍の派遣を決定、1991年1月にイラクを空爆して始まった戦争。 **set oneself up for~**「自分で〜のお膳立てをする」

Questions for Understanding

Look at the following statements. Write T if the statement is True, and F if it is False. Write the number of the paragraph where you find the answer in the parenthesis.

1. _____ According to the passage, Plato believed that our emotions caused us to make bad decisions. (#   )

2. _____ Wolfram Schultz discovered a connection between our experiences and our emotions. (#   )

3. _____ According to the passage, the radar officer made the wrong choice. (#   )

4. _____ According to the passage, the more information we have, the better decisions we make. (#   )

5. _____ According to the passage, the first step to making better decisions is understanding how we think. (#   )

Summary

Fill each space with the best word from the list below.

| separate   experiments   despite   overwhelmed   neuroscientists   confirm |

It is surprising how little we know about how we make decisions, 1)_____ making hundreds of them every day. It is only recently that 2)_____ have discovered that we use two 3)_____ systems to make decisions. One is rational thought, and the other is an emotional "gut feeling." Surprisingly, 4)_____ have shown that rational thought can easily be 5)_____ by too much information. In other words, when we need to make a tough choice, it is often better to focus on the option that feels right, and then use the available information to 6)_____ or reject our decision.

Chapter 7 Choices, Choices—How to Make Better Decisions

DATA ANALYSIS

Use the information in the passage to complete the table below.

Choosing a holiday destination for you and your friend.

Buying a new computer.

Who do you talk to on your first day in a new class?

Choosing a new cell phone.

Choosing what to have for breakfast.

Answering a True or False question.

Choosing a holiday destination for you.

Preparing a study schedule.

Writing a shopping list.

Choosing a new pet.

Rational Decisions	Emotional Decisions

35

CHAPTER 8
There's No Such Thing as Trash
How Innovators Turn Rubbish into a Resource

GETTING READY ① 67

Choose the correct word or phrase from the list below to complete the story.

1. A company in Turkey has invented a way to be _____ friendly and feed stray dogs at the same time.

2. When someone _____ a plastic bottle in their specially designed machine, some dog food is dispensed.

3. The bottles are recycled to pay for the dog food and undrunk water is also provided to the animals. This provides _____ benefits to the animals and the environment.

4. This _____ is said to have helped over 150,000 stray cats and dogs in Istanbul.

5. This is a very good example of how a clever idea can provide a _____ solution to a city's problems.

considerable   innovation   throws away   environmentally   long-lasting

READING ① 68~73

1 CD 68 The three Rs of the environment, Reduce, Reuse, and Recycle, give us clear guidelines about how we can change our behavior to benefit the environment. Once we have reduced what we buy, reduced packaging, and reduced what we throw away, we then think about reusing items and recycling them. Thinking
5 about the three Rs, we can come to realize that perhaps there is no such thing as rubbish. Almost everything we use and then discard can be turned into something else which is useful. Our desire to reuse and recycle, plus the considerable impact it can have environmentally, socially, and economically, has led to a great deal of innovation in this area.

Chapter 8 There's No Such Thing as Trash — How Innovators Turn Rubbish into a Resource

2 An exceptional example of recycling occurred in the West African country of Togo. An inventor, called Kodjo Afate Gnikou, managed to collect various discarded printer parts and computer circuit boards he found in junk yards. By using his imagination and talent, he combined the various items and with just a small investment of 100 dollars was able to create a 3D printer. The price was a fraction of what it would have cost to buy a new one. This is just one example that shows how, with a little insight and creativity, we can obtain a great deal of value from the things we throw away.

For most people, a mountain of trash like this is just rubbish. But for some people, this is a mountain of opportunities.

3 It is amazing what can be done with recycled materials. Soft drink bottles, often called PET bottles, are one of the most versatile items for recycling. PET bottles can be recycled into a wide range of useful items such as new PET bottles and containers, carpet and clothing, rope, upholstery fabrics, sails, parts for cars, filling for winter jackets and sleeping bags, and construction materials. They can also be made into pens. The brand Begreen, which was developed by the well-known Pilot brand, has launched a pen called B2P (bottle to pen) of which 89 percent is made from plastic bottles. They claim that the pen is the first recycled pen to be made from the material. There is also a Spanish company, founded by Javier Goyeneche, called Fun&Basics. The company produces a trolley bag by recycling 84 PET bottles. They developed a new approach to manufacturing which is embodied in the brand ECOALF. ECOALF makes products which are made from recycled materials, and they are now creating a range of fashionable recycled bags from this new material as well as clothing and swimwear. One of the most remarkable uses is the case of the artist, Richart Sowa, who used 100,000 PET bottles to make his own floating island called Joyxee, which floats in the seas near Cancun in Mexico. The island boasts a two-bedroom house, beaches, mangroves, a coral reef, its own Internet connection, and even a goat. The creator describes the island as something that is made out of trash but which has become a treasure.

4 One of the most far-reaching and impactful projects using recycled PET

37

bottles is the so-called "liter of light" project. A plastic bottle is filled with water and a little bleach to prevent algae, fitted to the roof of a house and then exposed to the sun. This bottle then becomes a source of daytime light as the water in the bottle refracts the light into the interior space. Its inventor, a Brazilian named Alfredo Moser, says that a bottle can provide the same amount of light as a traditional 40 to 60 watt electric light bulb and lasts for up to five years. In the Philippines, this has helped thousands of people as many have no access to electricity. The light is currently used in around 15 countries including Argentina, Fiji, Botswana, India, and Bangladesh.

5 The ideas of reuse and recycling are spreading into many areas of life. It is even possible to build a recycled home. A company called Earthship Biotecture has been developing these homes since the 1970s with the aim of using recycled materials and so reducing the carbon footprint of the houses they build. They are built from recycled materials such as tires filled with earth (in Britain, 48 million tires are thrown away each year), glass bottles and drink cans. Another example is the house built by Bruce Campbell in Oregon from an old Boeing 727 airplane that was going to be turned into scrap metal. Between 500 and 600 planes are retired annually and they would otherwise sit in scrapyards and get turned into scrap metal. Bruce Campbell is planning to build his next house, using a retired Boeing 747, in Japan.

6 The next time you buy something, reflect carefully on whether you do actually need it and make sure it has as little packaging as possible if you do. When you are thinking of throwing something away, think about whether it can be used in a different way or be recycled to make something else. If you change your thinking, you will be surprised at how little trash you actually need to create.

NOTES

there's no such thing as ~「～など（存在し）ない」　　**rubbish**「ごみ，がらくた，廃棄物」　**dispense**「給餌する，分与する」　**long-lasting**「長期にわたる，長続きする」　**Togo**「トーゴ共和国」西アフリカの共和制国家　　**Kodjo Afate Gnikou**「コジョ・アファテ・ニコ」彼が製作した3Dプリンターは「W. Afate」と名付けられた。　**circuit boards**「回路基板，サーキットボード」　**junkyard**「廃品投棄場，がらくた部品置き場」　**3D printer** Chapter 9のNotesを参照　**fraction**「(全体に対して) 一部, 小部分, 断片」 **at a fraction of the cost**「ほんのわずかな費用で」　**upholstery**「内装飾品」　　**Begreen**「ビグリーン」筆記具で知られる株式会社パイロットコーポレーション（Pilot＝本社東京）の環境配慮商品のブランド。　　**Javier Goyeneche**「ハビエル・ゴジェネチェ」スペインのブランド Fun & Basics（ファン＆ベーシック）の創業者。　　**trolley bag**「底部に車輪が付いたかばん，キャリーバッグ」　　**ECOALF**「エコアルフ」ゴジェネチェ氏が手がけたブランド　　**Cancun**「カンクン」メキシコ東部のカリブ海沿岸にある都市　　**coral reef**「サンゴ礁」　**far-reaching**「広範囲にわたる，遠大な」　　**algae** (pl.)「藻，藻類に属する植物」単数形は alga　**carbon footprint**「二酸化炭素排出量」

Chapter 8   There's No Such Thing as Trash — How Innovators Turn Rubbish into a Resource

QUESTIONS FOR UNDERSTANDING

Check the best answer for each question.

1. What is the main conclusion we can draw from employing the three Rs?
    a. ☐ Innovation is the only way we may successfully employ the three Rs.
    b. ☐ The three Rs programs will never be successful without government support.
    c. ☐ Our attitude to what is and what is not trash may change as a result of the three Rs.
    d. ☐ Guidelines have not been very successful in encouraging people to take up the three Rs.

2. What can we learn from the example of Kodjo Afate Gnikou?
    a. ☐ We are all missing opportunities to recycle seemingly useless items into useful, valuable things.
    b. ☐ A great deal of investment is still necessary to make useful things from trash.
    c. ☐ Unless you have special access to high-tech facilities, it is impossible to produce something like Gnikou's 3D printer.
    d. ☐ It would be a good idea to start charging for recyclable items that can be found in junk yards.

3. According to the passage, what items can be made from recycled PET bottles?
    a. ☐ pens, bags, printers, and trolleys
    b. ☐ islands, pens, sleeping bags, and furniture
    c. ☐ islands, pens, swimwear, and car parts
    d. ☐ carpet, rope, construction materials, and winter jackets

4. Why is the "liter of light" project so significant?
    a. ☐ It is an amazingly cheap way to light an interior space.
    b. ☐ It was invented by a poor man from Brazil and not a large company.
    c. ☐ It has had far-reaching social and economic benefits in poor countries.
    d. ☐ The light can last up to five years.

SUMMARY

Fill each space with the best word or phrase from the list below.

> a range   behavior   treasure   inventors   remarkable   entrepreneurs

The three Rs give us an excellent starting point for how we might modify our 1)_____ in order to benefit the environment. It is 2)_____ how much human invention and innovation has been focused on this area in recent years. There are 3)_____ building 3D printers from junk, companies manufacturing successful products from PET bottles, and even people constructing their own ecological islands and recycled homes. However, we do not have to be gifted 4)_____ to participate in this movement. There is 5)_____ of measures anyone can undertake to help ourselves and the environment. Perhaps sometime soon we can all realize the dream that Richart Sowa seeks to attain: turning trash into 6)_____.

CHAPTER 9

Printing the Future
How 3D Printing Is Changing the World

GETTING READY

Choose the correct word or phrase from the list below to complete the story.

1. African inventor Kodjo Afate Gnikou _____ the adage, "Waste not, want not," _____.

2. The 3D printers he saw _____ were too expensive for people in Togo to buy.

3. So he decided to make his own. He gathered _____ from junk yards near his home.

4. This _____ him to build a 3D printer for less than $100.

5. He wants to show the world that Africa is also part of this new technological _____.

| keeps ... in mind | advance | material | allowed | for sale |

READING

1 Two technologies that completely changed our world are printing and computers. Printing allowed knowledge to be quickly and accurately copied and changed reading into a regular hobby instead of a luxury. Computers have become common in every part of our lives. They are our offices, entertainment systems, and our shops. Now, printing and computing are coming together to create a 5
new technology that will revolutionize our way of life—additive manufacturing, popularly known as 3D printing.

2 What is 3D printing? Imagine that you print a large exclamation point "!" on a page. Now imagine that you print it again and again in the same place. When you rub your fingers over the page, you will be able to feel the exclamation 10
point because of the many layers of ink you have printed. This is 3D printing.

However, 3D exclamation points on a sheet of paper are not so useful. The 3D printers being used by scientists and companies do not print with ink. Instead, they print with plastic, metal, concrete, and even human cells. How will this incredible new technology affect our lives?

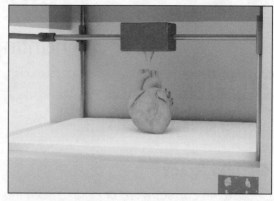

This human heart is made of plastic, but doctors are already using 3D printers to print simple human body parts.

3 **Shopping**: The speed and convenience of online shopping have made it commonplace in under ten years. 3D printing will make some forms of online shopping even faster. Instead of browsing for a product, ordering it, and then waiting for it to be delivered, you will download the design, perhaps customize it a little, and then print it on your home 3D printer. In addition, anyone will be able to upload designs of their own, whether for free or for sale.

4 **Space travel:** It is not often that shopping, the world's favorite hobby, and space exploration share the same technology, but 3D printing is one exception. In August 2013, NASA successfully tested a part for a rocket engine that had been 3D-printed. Unlike the regular design, which had 115 parts, the 3D-printed version had only two parts. As a result, it was stronger and cost 80 percent less than the regular design. In September 2014, NASA sent a 3D printer to the International Space Station to test 3D printing tools and spare parts. In future space missions, being able to make tools and parts when they are needed could mean the difference between life and death in an emergency.

5 **Construction:** Not all 3D printers are small. In 2014, an American architect designed a small castle and then spent six months 3D printing it in concrete in his back yard. Also in 2014, a Chinese company 3D-printed ten small houses near Shanghai in a single day. These houses are designed for use after emergencies such as earthquakes, so producing them quickly is important. In Amsterdam, the 3D Print Canal House is a project to 3D print a traditional style Dutch canal house using recycled materials. Space agencies such as NASA are very interested in construction with 3D printing because it could be used to build bases on other planets in the future.

Chapter 9 Printing the Future—How 3D Printing Is Changing the World

6 **Medicine:** Doctors can already do amazing things using 3D printers. Here are just a few examples. In 2013, surgeons at Boston Children's Hospital used a 3D-printed model of a child's brain to plan a ten-hour operation. Doctors also use 3D printers to produce replacement body parts. In 2014, Chinese surgeons 3D-printed replacement metal vertebrae for a 12-year-old boy, Dutch surgeons 3D-printed a plastic skull to repair a woman's damaged one, and Welsh surgeons 3D-printed replacement plastic bones to rebuild a man's face. However, in the future doctors would like to be able to print replacement organs and bones using human cells. Already it is possible to create short blood vessels and small amounts of cartilage and skin, and it is hoped that the first 3D-printed organs will be produced by 2030.

7 However, the ability of 3D printers to print nearly anything means we must consider their use very carefully. For example, in May 2013, the American group Defense Distributed released a design for a single-shot pistol. In July 2013, a Canadian uploaded a rifle design, and in August 2013, an American gunsmith uploaded a five-shot pistol design. In May 2014, a Japanese man was arrested for possessing six 3D-printed guns, including a six-shot revolver he had designed himself.

8 3D printing could be good for the environment, reducing waste and cutting energy use as we produce the goods we need, when we need them, and recycle our unwanted things. This future promises enormous advances in medicine and will encourage us to design and share new goods and ideas. Already, nearly 20 percent of U.S. libraries have 3D printers that anyone can use. However, 3D printers also make it harder for the police and governments to control dangerous goods like weapons. Being able to create any product we like does not mean that we should do so. We should keep the old adage, "With great power comes great responsibility," firmly in mind when we consider our 3D-printed future.

NOTES

3D printer「3Dプリンター」立体物のデータから、樹脂などを加工してその立体物を造形する装置。3D（3次元）の設計データを入力すれば、印刷する感覚で立体物が製作できる。**adage**「ことわざ，格言」 **keep ~ in mind**「〜を心にとめる，覚えておく，肝に命じる」 **customize**「好み（必要）に合わせて改造・変更する，カスタマイズする」 **upload**「アップロードする」周辺・下位のコンピューターから、中央・上位のコンピューターにデータやプログラムを送信すること。個々のパソコンからインターネットのサーバーに送ることを意味することが多い。cf. download **International Space Station** (the ~)「国際宇宙ステーション」地上約400キロ上空に建設された巨大な有人実験施設。地球一周を約90分というスピードで回っている。米国、日本、カナダ、ロシア、欧州各国の計15カ国が協力して計画を推進し、宇宙での特殊な環境を利用した実験や研究、地球や天体の観測を行うことを目的としている。2000年から宇宙飛行士が滞在を開始し、現在は6カ月ごとに交代している。 **vertebrae** (pl.) > vertebra「椎骨，脊椎骨」 **Welsh**「ウェールズの、ウェールズ人（語）の」英国の正式名称はUnited Kingdom of Great Britain and Northern Irelandで、イングランド、スコットランド、ウェールズ、北アイルランドから構成される。 **blood vessel**「血管」 **cartilage**「軟骨」 **Defense Distributed**「ディフェンス・ディストリビューテッド」米国テキサス州の非営利団体。「3Dプリンター銃」の普及プロジェクトを行い物議を醸している。ライフル銃などの主要部品の設計図を開発してインターネット上で公開、世界中の誰でも自由にダウンロードして部品を複製できるようにした。3Dプリンターで製作した部品を使用した銃も本物同様に発砲できることから、波紋が広がっている。 **single-shot**「単発の」 **pistol**「拳銃，ピストル」 **rifle**「ライフル銃，小銃」通常は拳銃などは含まず、肩にかけるタイプの銃身の長い小銃を指すことが多い。 **revolver**「輪胴式拳銃，リボルバー」

QUESTIONS FOR UNDERSTANDING

Look at the following statements. Write T if the statement is True, and F if it is False. Write the number of the paragraph where you find the answer in the parenthesis.

1. _____ The invention of the computer means we can copy knowledge quickly. (#   )

2. _____ In the future, spacecraft may be produced using 3D printers. (#   )

3. _____ Boston Children's Hospital created a child's brain using a 3D printer. (#   )

4. _____ It is already possible to use 3D printers to make guns. (#   )

5. _____ Nearly one in five American libraries prints books using 3D printers. (#   )

Chapter 9 Printing the Future—How 3D Printing Is Changing the World

Summary

Fill each space with the best word or phrase from the list below.

> upload   exploration   browse   in an emergency   customize   organs

When we 1)_____ for books in a bookstore or online, it is easy to forget how much printing and computers have changed our world. Now the two technologies have combined and our lives will never be the same again. 3D printing will allow shoppers to 2)_____ the things they buy so that they are truly individual and unique. Furthermore, everyone will be able to 3)_____ and share their own designs. 4)_____ such as an earthquake, rescuers will be able to print the tools and equipment they need, as well as shelter for the victims. Surgeons will be able to print replacement 5)_____, and space 6)_____ will be simple when astronauts can print their own spaceships.

Data Analysis

Complete the timeline for 3D-printed guns with information from the passage.

Deadly Designs

May 2013	A design for a _____ is released.
July 2013	A _____ is uploaded.
August 2013	A _____ design is released.
May 2014	A Japanese man designs a _____.

45

CHAPTER 10

Tuesday's Child Is Full of Grace
Does Your Birthday Affect Your Life?

GETTING READY ① 85

Choose the correct word or phrase from the list below to complete the story.

1. How does the weather _____ you? Does it make you happy or sad when it is hot and sunny?

2. For many years, scientists thought that mood was not _____ weather. However, in 2011 scientists found that the weather does have an impact on our mood, but only for about half of us.

3. Of the rest, nearly 30 percent said that warmth and sunshine made them feel happy. About 10 percent of people felt bad when it rained, and around 10 percent of people have a form of _____ in the winter.

4. They _____ tiredness, sadness, and an increased risk of suicide.

5. Perhaps the most surprising discovery was the _____ that nearly 10 percent of people felt the same about the summer.

> suffer from   observation   depression   affect   connected with

READING ① 86~93

1 CD 86

Monday's child is fair of face,
Tuesday's child is full of grace,
Wednesday's child is full of woe,
Thursday's child has far to go,
5   Friday's child is loving and giving,
Saturday's child works hard for a living,
But the child who is born on the Sabbath Day
Is happy and wise and good and gay.

                    A 15th century English poem

Chapter 10 Tuesday's Child Is Full of Grace—Does Your Birthday Affect Your Life?

A summer birthday party. Nearly three quarters of babies are born between spring and fall.

2 When is your birthday? Do you know what day of the week it was? How about the time? For thousands of years, astrologers have tried to predict our health, personality, and destiny based on the time and date we were born. In the Chinese *Zi Wei Dou Shu* system, five different elements (Metal, Wood, Water, Fire, and Earth) are connected with five planets (Venus, Jupiter, Mercury, Mars, and Saturn), and the planets' position in one of 28 different constellations of stars when you are born is used to predict your future. In Europe, North America, and India, a mixture of ancient Babylonian and Egyptian astrology is used. This system connects the time of your birth with the position of the same five planets, plus the Sun and the Moon, in 12 different constellations of stars.

3 These astrological systems are so different that they both cannot be right, but which one is wrong? During the 20th century, scientists in many different countries studied astrology to see how effective it was. The scientists discovered that the predictions made by astrologers using the Chinese system were no better than just guessing. European and Indian astrology do not work either. And yet, throughout history, people have noticed that the date of your birth has an effect on your life. If astrology does not work, can science explain these observations?

4 In order to discover if the time of our birth has an effect on our lives, scientists need to collect information about the lives of many thousands of people and compare it with when they were born. This kind of massive data analysis could not be done until recently because it requires very powerful computers to process the data.

5 Perhaps the first discovery made is that most babies are born in the summer and fall. In the United States between 1973 and 1999, nearly 70 percent of babies were born between May and October, and only 30 percent between November and April. The opposite pattern is seen in Australia, where the seasons are reversed. This pattern of births can have a big impact on education, especially at elementary school. For example, if the school year begins in September, such as in the United States and Britain, children born between September and December do better than children born between January and April, and children born between May and August do the worst. Why? The simple answer is that if a child born in September and a child born in August are in the same class, the child who was born in September will be nearly one year older than the child born in August. When you realize that, it is easy to see how your birthday could affect your educational performance.

6 As well as education, other effects that result from the season we are born in have been discovered. Babies born in the winter are more likely to start crawling earlier than babies born in the summer. They are also less likely to be short-sighted. However, people born in the winter are also more likely to suffer from allergies, schizophrenia, depression, and eating disorders. On the other hand, people born in the summer are more likely to commit suicide than people born in the winter.

7 What could cause these differences? One of the biggest differences between winter and summer is the amount of sunlight. Our bodies use sunlight to make vitamin D, and it is possible that changes in the amount of vitamin D in women's bodies when they are pregnant are the reason for some of these differences. Another possible reason is that the food we eat in the summer and the food we eat in the winter is often different, and this could affect how babies grow before they are born.

8 While it is clear that our time of birth *can* affect our health, we should probably not be too worried. British scientists needed to analyze the data from 60,000 people in order to discover that eight percent of people born in the winter suffer from eating disorders while seven percent of people born in the summer do. In other words, these effects are very small. The positive benefits of a good diet, regular exercise, and avoiding tobacco and alcohol are much bigger. One thing is clear—our destiny is most definitely *not* decided by our birth date.

NOTES

Monday's child is fair of face, ... 英詩。作者不詳。一般に「マザーグースの詩」の一つとして知られるが、書かれたのは15世紀「マザーグース」は、ロンドンの出版業者ジョン・ニューベリーが1765年ごろに刊行した「マザーグースのメロディー」(Mother Goose Melodies) に由来する。 **Sabbath Day**「安息日」仕事を休み、祈りと休息に当てる日。旧約聖書「創世記」で神が6日間の創造を完了し、7日目に休息したことにちなむ。一般にユダヤ教では土曜日、キリスト教では日曜日。 **astrologer**「占星術師」 **Zi Wei Dou Shu**「紫微斗数」中国独特の占術。生年月日時を基に運勢を占う。 **ancient Babylonian astrology**「古代バビロニアの占星術」バビロニアはチグリス・ユーフラテス両河下流域を占めた古代メソポタミアの南東部にあった王国で、現在のイラク南部に当たる。紀元前3100年ごろから紀元後1世紀にかけて、バビロニアではさまざまなテーマの文書が楔形文字で書かれた。その中には占星術や天文学に関するものもあり、近代的な天文学や現代

Chapter 10   Tuesday's Child Is Full of Grace—Does Your Birthday Affect Your Life?

の星座占いなども、その起源は古代バビロニアにさかのぼる。バビロニアでの占星術の発達は、イエス・キリストの誕生を知らせる星を観測した「東方の三博士」の聖書の記述からもうかがえる。
ancient Egyptian astrology「古代エジプトの占星術」古代エジプトはローマに征服されるまでのエジプトを指し、おそらく世界最古で最長の王制を維持していた。紀元前3000年ごろに始まった第一王朝から、紀元前332年にアレクサンドロス大王に滅ぼされるまでを指す。　**process** (v.)「(データを) 処理する」　**schizophrenia**「統合失調症」

QUESTIONS FOR UNDERSTANDING

Check the best answer for each question.

1. According to the passage, what did scientists discover about astrology?
   a. ☐ They found that Chinese astrology was accurate, but that European astrology was not.
   b. ☐ They found that Indian astrology was accurate, but that European astrology was not.
   c. ☐ They found that European astrology was accurate, but that Chinese astrology was not.
   d. ☐ They found that all forms of astrology were inaccurate.

2. What did scientists discover about babies born in Australia?
   a. ☐ They found that nearly 70 percent of babies were born between May and October, and only 30 percent between November and April.
   b. ☐ They found that nearly 70 percent of babies were born between November and April, and only 30 percent between May and October.
   c. ☐ They found that nearly 50 percent of babies were born between May and October, and nearly 50 percent between November and April.
   d. ☐ They found that 70 percent more babies were born in the United States than in Australia between 1973 and 1999.

3. According to the passage, what is the most likely explanation for seasonal differences between people?
   a. ☐ Women are exposed to different amounts of sunlight and have different allergies in different seasons.
   b. ☐ Women are exposed to different amounts of sunlight and vitamin D in different seasons.
   c. ☐ Women are exposed to different amounts of sunlight and eat different foods in different seasons.
   d. ☐ Women are exposed to different amounts of sunlight and have different eating disorders in different seasons.

4. What does the study by British scientists tell us about the effect of when we are born on our lives?
   a. ☐ That whether we will have an eating disorder or not depends on when we were born.
   b. ☐ That people born in the winter need to have different diets and exercise plans than people born in the summer.
   c. ☐ That people born in the spring and autumn have no chance to suffer from eating disorders.
   d. ☐ That the impact of when we were born is much less important than what we do afterwards.

SUMMARY

Fill each space with the best word or phrase from the list below.

| no better than   constellation   result from   disorders   be worried   avoid |

To believe in astrology is to believe that someone can look at a 1)_____ of stars in the sky and predict your personality and future. The reality is that consulting an astrologer is 2)_____ guessing. However, scientists have discovered that when we are born *can* influence how likely we are to suffer from 3)_____ such as depression and schizophrenia. These effects 4)_____ the diet our mothers ate and the amount of sunlight they experienced when they were pregnant. Should we 5)_____ by these findings? Not really. The effects are very small, and we can benefit from this knowledge by taking steps that will help us 6)_____ ever suffering from these problems.

CHAPTER 11

A Good Night's Sleep
Why Do We Need to Sleep?

GETTING READY

② 02

Choose the correct word from the list below to complete the story.

1. Throughout history, the moon has been connected to sleep and madness. _____ such as Aristotle thought that the full moon made people mad because it stopped them from sleeping.

2. In 2013, scientists investigated the effect of the moon on sleep. They discovered that people took an extra five minutes to fall _____ on nights with a full moon.

3. Furthermore, they discovered that people slept for an _____ of 20 minutes less on nights with a full moon.

4. The scientists believe that the light from the moon reduces the amount of a _____ in our brains called melatonin, which controls when we sleep and when we wake up.

5. As a result, we spend more time _____ when the moon is full.

| asleep | awake | average | chemical | philosophers |

READING

② 03~09

1 ᶜᴰ 03 Think about your day yesterday. How much of it can you remember? You can probably remember quite a lot about what you did, where you went, and what you ate. However, there is almost certainly a big hole in your memory—can you remember what happened when you were asleep? We spend about one third of our lives sleeping. In other words, by the time you are 21 years old, you have probably spent seven years asleep. Can you remember any of that time? Why do we sleep? Why do we remember so little of our sleeping lives? Do we really need to sleep? Philosophers and artists have searched for the answers to these questions for centuries without success. But in recent years, science has started to uncover amazing facts about sleep.

2 It is not only humans that sleep. All mammals sleep, and so do birds, reptiles, insects, and even most kinds of fish. However, the length of time that animals sleep can be very different. While humans generally sleep for between six and ten hours every day, animals such as horses, cows, elephants, and giraffes only sleep for three or four hours a day. Our pets like to sleep longer, with dogs sleeping for an average of ten hours a day, and cats sleeping for an average of 12 hours a day. However, some kinds of bat sleep for nearly 20 hours every day. What can explain these huge differences? One answer is the kind of food these animals eat. Horses and cows eat plants, which are difficult to digest. As a result, they must spend more of their time awake and eating. Dogs and cats eat meat, which contains more energy than plants. This means that they need to spend less time finding food. Small animals such as bats need a lot of energy, so they use as little energy as possible when they are not hunting. This is why they sleep so much.

Cats can sleep for 12 hours every day. How much sleep did YOU have last night?

3 The way different animals sleep can also be different to humans. When we sleep, our whole brains sleep. However, in birds, reptiles and some mammals such as dolphins, which live in water, only half of the brain sleeps at one time. This allows the animals to fly or swim underwater safely.

4 The fact that so many different kinds of animal sleep tells us that sleep is very important, and also that sleeping is a very old behavior. So what happens if we do not sleep? For many animals, missing sleep can be deadly. For humans, the effects are usually much less severe, however. In 1964, Rand Gardner, a 17-year-old American, stayed awake for 11 days and 24 minutes. At the end of this period, his memory and concentration had become very bad. He was also suffering from hallucinations—he was seeing and hearing things that were not real. However, after sleeping for more than 25 hours over the next two days, he recovered completely.

5 So why do we need to sleep? When we sleep, the most active parts of our bodies such as our digestive system shut down. We also use much less energy than we do when we are awake. This allows our bodies to repair damage, fight infections, heal wounds, and remove dangerous chemicals and substances. Perhaps more important is what happens in our brains. Sleep is when our brains construct our long-term memories. This is one reason why dreams often seem to jump between ideas and events. It is because our brains are connecting our recent experiences and thoughts with older ones to create strong new memories. This connection between sleep and memory is why sleeping on a problem can help us to solve it…and is also why staying up late to study before a test is a really bad idea.

6 So how much sleep do we need? Not getting the right amount of sleep over a long period of time can lead to serious health problems and can even shorten our lives. Not having enough sleep can result in memory and concentration problems, poor decision making, and weight gain. It can also weaken our immune systems, slow down our healing, and increase our risk of developing diabetes, depression, schizophrenia, and heart disease. Getting too much sleep also leads to weight gain and an increased risk of heart disease and Alzheimer's disease. The optimum number of hours of sleep for an adult is between six and eight hours a day. However, teenagers need a little longer, requiring between eight and ten hours a day. This discovery should make us think carefully about when school should start in the morning and how late students should be made to study in the evening.

7 In our modern world, sleeping for nearly one third of every day can seem like a waste of valuable time that can be better used for work, study, and play. Science has shown us that getting the right balance of activity and sleep is essential for our long term physical and mental health. Truly, the ancient poet Homer was right when he said, "There is a time for many words, and there is also a time for sleep."

NOTES

a good night's sleep「十分な睡眠，ぐっすり眠ること」 **Aristotle**「アリストテレス（384-322 B.C.E.）」古代ギリシアの哲学者。プラトンの弟子。 **melatonin**「メラトニン」脊椎動物の松果体で作られ分泌されるホルモン。ヒトでは睡眠を促進する効果があるとされる。 **reptile**「爬虫（はちゅう）類」 **underwater**「水面下で，水中で」 **long-term memory**「長期記憶」cf. short-term memory **stay up late**「夜更かしする」 **immune system**「免疫システム，免疫系」 **diabetes**「糖尿病」 **depression**「鬱病，抑鬱症」 **schizophrenia**「統合失調症」 **Alzheimer's disease**「アルツハイマー病」 **optimum**「最善の，最適な，(ある条件下での) 最上の」 **Homer**「ホメロス，ホメーロス」紀元前9〜8世紀ごろの古代ギリシアの詩人。叙事詩『イリアッド』(Iliad) と『オデュッセイア（オデッセイ）』(Odyssey) の作者といわれる。"There is a time for many words, and there is also a time for sleep."『オデュッセイア』第11歌より

Questions for Understanding

Look at the following statements. Write T if the statement is True, and F if it is False. Write the number of the paragraph where you find the answer in the parenthesis.

1. _____ According to the passage, we spend about one third of our lives awake. (#)
2. _____ According to the passage, animals that eat meat generally need less sleep than animals that eat plants. (#)
3. _____ Scientists have discovered that sleep starts in one half of the brain and then moves to the other half. (#)
4. _____ According to the passage, one reason we need to sleep is to construct memories. (#)
5. _____ According to the passage, it is better to sleep for too long than to sleep too little. (#)

Summary

Fill each space with the best word or phrase from the list below.

| result in | wounds | diabetes | ancient | behavior | weaken |

Sleep is a 1)_____ that we share with nearly all other animals, from insects to reptiles. This tells us that sleep is both 2)_____ and important. We now know that sleep allows our brains to construct memories and our bodies to heal 3)_____. Not getting enough sleep can 4)_____ our immune systems and can 5)_____ longer lasting infections and deadly diseases such as 6)_____. Sleep is important for our health and well-being, and we should ensure that we get the right amount every night.

Chapter 11 A Good Night's Sleep—Why Do We Need to Sleep?

DATA ANALYSIS

Use the information in the passage to complete the table using the words below.

~~poor decision making~~ ~~heart disease (x2)~~ hallucinations poor memory

poor concentration weak immune system slow healing diabetes

depression schizophrenia weight gain (x2) Alzheimer's disease

	Short-term effects	Long-term effects
Too little sleep	Poor decision making	Heart disease
Too much sleep		Heart disease

Chapter 12

Space Age Gold Rush
Asteroid Mining

Getting Ready

Choose the correct word from the list below to complete the story.

1. The European Space Agency's Rosetta _____ began on March 2, 2004.

2. After its _____, Rosetta first traveled to Mars.

3. After that, it visited the _____ 21 Lutetia and 2867 Šteins.

4. On November 12, 2014 Rosetta's Philae lander became the first _____ to land on a comet.

5. It took ten years and ten months to _____ this goal.

> asteroids   launch   spacecraft   mission   achieve

Reading

1 Space travel and exploration present many challenges to humanity. There is no air in space, the temperatures can freeze or cook us, and the level of radiation can be dangerously high. In addition, the lack of gravity can make our bones weak and our hearts smaller. Beyond these physical problems is the
5 loneliness of space. It took only three days to fly to the Moon, but it would take six months to fly to Mars. That means that a mission to Mars could last for a year or more. Imagine spending that much time in a small room with just a few other people. Could you stand it? Furthermore, if anything went wrong, there would be no chance of a rescue.

10 **2** However, all of these human challenges can be met. We can build spacecraft that keep the passengers safe. We can develop exercise machines and routines that keep astronauts' bodies strong. And we can choose only the best trained and mentally fit people for long missions. In fact, one of the biggest challenges

we face is the technological one of getting into space.

3 [CD 14] The problem is fuel. The Lunar Module used by the Apollo astronauts weighed up to 45,000kg including the fuel it needed to fly to the Moon and back. The rocket that launched it into space needed enough fuel to lift the Lunar Module into space against the Earth's gravity. However, that fuel also weighed a lot, so more fuel was needed to lift it. That meant that a bigger rocket was needed to hold the extra fuel, and a bigger rocket was heavier, so it needed even more fuel to lift it. The Saturn V rocket used for the Apollo missions weighed three million kilograms. In other words, 85 percent of the mass of an Apollo Moon mission was used just to get the astronauts into space. The Apollo astronauts only needed a week of supplies. A mission to Mars might need two years of supplies. That means even bigger rockets, or lots of smaller launches just for one mission. All this fuel is expensive, it costs about $20,000 to lift one kilogram into space. But what if there was a different way?

Mining asteroids like this one could make exploring space much easier in the future.

4 [CD 15] If we could make fuel in space, then we could use much smaller rockets from Earth. If we could build spacecraft in space, then we would only need to send the astronauts into space, something we can do now with quite small rockets. How could this be achieved? American companies like Planetary Resources and Deep Space Industries plan to mine asteroids for the resources we need. They plan to use solar power to turn water ice into the best kind of rocket fuel, liquid hydrogen and liquid oxygen. The oxygen could also be used to provide air for astronauts to breathe, and water is essential for life as well as for many industrial processes.

5 [CD 16] Their plans do not stop there. As well as ice, asteroids contain metals including iron, nickel, and platinum. All of these metals are valuable on Earth, and are essential in building spacecraft. Deep Space Industries is developing a 3D printer that will work in space so that spacecraft and satellites can be built in space using materials that are already there. Although this work is at a very early stage, already NASA has sent a 3D printer to the International Space Station to test the technology.

6 However, there are several problems. One is that no one knows if asteroids have enough water ice and metals to make mining them worthwhile. Starting in 2015, Planetary Resources plans to launch a series of small space telescopes to identify asteroids that are worth mining. Another problem is that asteroid mining will probably need to rely on robots, but robots are not reliable or sophisticated enough to automatically mine asteroids. There is a third problem. According to the 1967 United Nations Outer Space Treaty, "the exploration and use of outer space shall be carried out for the benefit of all countries and shall be the province of all mankind." That means that nations cannot say that they own a planet or an asteroid. It also means that companies cannot claim them either.

7 If humanity wants to continue to explore space, we must find a way of building spacecraft and making fuel in space. One possible way to do that is to mine asteroids, but in the current economic situation, national governments do not want to spend the enormous amount of money this would cost. It may be that, in order to conquer space, humanity will need to compromise its ideals and allow private companies to make money from mining and selling space rocks.

NOTES

gold rush「ゴールドラッシュ」新しく発見された金産地に一獲千金を狙って採掘者が殺到すること。1849年の米国カリフォルニア州でのゴールドラッシュが有名。 **asteroid**（=planetoid, minor planet)「小惑星」火星の軌道と木星の軌道との間、およびその付近に散在する。 **mining**「採鉱，鉱業，採掘」 **asteroid mining**「小惑星鉱業」小惑星にある鉱物資源を採掘・開発すること **European Space Agency**「欧州宇宙機関（ESA）」本部をフランス・パリに置く国際共同機関。欧州では各国、特に英国やフランスで独自に宇宙開発を行っていたが、米国や旧ソ連に対抗し、より効果的な欧州宇宙開発活動を実現するために、1975年にESAが設立された。独立機関だが、欧州連合（EU）と密接な協力関係をもつ。 **Rosetta**「ロゼッタ」ESAによる彗星探査ミッション。彗星は太陽系初期から存在し現在も当時の姿をとどめていると考えられており、太陽系の歴史を知るために彗星の探査を行うのが目的。彗星探査機は、周回機「ロゼッタ」と実験用小型着陸機「フィラエ（Philae）」で構成される。 **21 Lutetia and 2867 Šteins**「小惑星ルテティアと小惑星シュテインス」 **Lunar Module**「アポロ月着陸船」一般の「月着陸船」を意味する場合は大文字にせずlunar module と表記 **Apollo missions**「アポロ計画」米国による一連の月探査計画。1960年7月にアメリカ航空宇宙局（NASA）が計画を発表し、1969年に宇宙船アポロ11号が人類史上初めて有人で月面に着陸した。 **Planetary Resources**「プラネタリー・リソーシズ社」小惑星採掘を目指す米国のベンチャー企業 **Deep Space Industries**「ディープ・スペース・インダストリーズ社」米国のベンチャー企業。小惑星採掘を行い、採掘した資源で3Dプリンターを用いて宇宙で製品を作ることを目指している。 **liquid hydrogen and liquid oxygen**「液体水素と液体酸素」 **International Space Station** Chapter 9のNotesを参照 **space telescope**「宇宙望遠鏡」 **Outer Space Treaty**「(the ~) 宇宙条約」「月その他の天体を含む宇宙空間の探査及び利用における国家活動を律する原則に関する条約」の略称。平和利用の原則、領有の否定、軍事利用の禁止、国際協力などの宇宙利用に関する基本原則を定める。

Chapter 12 Space Age Gold Rush—Asteroid Mining

Questions for Understanding

Check the best answer for each question.

1. According to the passage, what is the biggest difficulty in sending people to Mars?
    a. ☐ A mission to Mars would need a huge amount of fuel and supplies.
    b. ☐ It would be impossible to rescue the astronauts if something went wrong.
    c. ☐ Space is a very dangerous place and the astronauts would all die.
    d. ☐ The astronauts would be very lonely and could go crazy.

2. Why do companies like Planetary Resources and Deep Space Industries want to mine asteroids?
    a. ☐ Because NASA wants them to supply the International Space Station.
    b. ☐ Because they want to use the 3D printer NASA sent to the International Space Station.
    c. ☐ Because they want to turn the ice and metals in asteroids into fuel, air, and spacecraft.
    d. ☐ Because they want to bring metals back to Earth and become rich.

3. Mining asteroids faces several challenges. Which of the following is **not** a challenge faced by these companies?
    a. ☐ International law means that companies cannot own asteroids.
    b. ☐ Current robot technology is not good enough to mine asteroids.
    c. ☐ NASA does not want private companies to mine asteroids.
    d. ☐ It is uncertain if asteroids contain enough useful metals and ice.

4. What does the passage suggest we might need to do if we want to encourage space exploration?
    a. ☐ We need to allow private companies to do business in space.
    b. ☐ We need to make sure our governments spend enough money on space travel.
    c. ☐ We need to make sure that the economic situation improves.
    d. ☐ We need to find new ways to build spacecraft.

Summary

Fill each space with the best word or phrase from the list below.

> breathe astronauts treaty in other words challenges essential

Space travel faces many 1)_____, but perhaps the greatest is getting into space to begin with. To send 2)_____ into outer space, we must lift their mass, their spacecraft's mass, and the mass of all of the fuel against gravity. 3)_____, it is very expensive to go into space. Asteroid mining could change that. By mining 4)_____ metals and water ice, private companies could build spacecraft in space and provide the oxygen we need to 5)_____. However, the current international space 6)_____ bans this kind of activity. If we truly want to conquer space, we will need to compromise and encourage business in space.

CHAPTER 13

Raising Money
The Crowdfunding Revolution

GETTING READY

Choose the correct word or phrase from the list below to complete the story.

1. The traditional way to _____ musical success is for a band to join a large music company.

2. But what can a band do if they do not want to _____ a contract with a music company?

3. In 2008, the Japanese rock band, Electric Eel Shock, needed to _____ to make their new album, *Sugoi Indeed*.

4. The band contacted their fans _____ and asked them for help. In only 55 days, the band received $50,000 from their fans around the world.

5. The success of Electric Eel Shock _____ how the Internet is changing the music industry.

| online | sign | raise money | demonstrates | achieve |

READING

1 The term "crowdfunding" is used to describe a method of raising money by using one of the nearly 500 crowdfunding websites on the Internet such as GoFundMe, Kickstarter, or IndieGoGo. The IndieGoGo website tells us that: "IndieGoGo empowers people to activate the global community to make ideas happen. Then, we help you spread the word." What does this mean? It means that if you have a business idea, an idea for a charity, if you want to make a movie, or if you have invented something new, people from around the world will help you to make those ideas become reality.

2 Crowdfunding can also be a lot more personal, which is the speciality of gofundme.com. On this site, you can give money to people who need help, such as to recover after an accident or unfortunate incident. Some people are even raising money for their dream honeymoon! Unlike many charities, gofundme.com allows people to choose exactly who they want to help. The crowdfunding idea has proved to be very successful and represents a new way that money is raised and used. Kickstarter, perhaps the largest crowdfunding site, has raised $1.55 billion since it began in 2009, and GoFundMe has raised $770 million for personal causes since it was launched in 2010.

Crowdfunding is a new way to raise money for business ideas.

3 What is special about crowdfunding? Traditionally, if you needed to borrow money to start a business, you only had a couple of options. The first of these was to borrow money from your family and friends. If you needed more money than your family or friends had, you could borrow money from a bank or try to find a professional investor. Both of these approaches have some problems. If your business fails, your family and friends will lose their money. If you borrow money from a bank or an investor, you may lose control of your own business. Crowdfunding allows you to present your idea via the Internet. Because this allows your idea to reach a lot of people, even if each person contributes a relatively small amount of money, you can still raise a lot of money to support your project. In other words, crowdfunding combines the best parts of the two traditional ways of borrowing money.

4 Of course, crowdfunding websites are businesses themselves. Crowdfunding websites charge fees based on the amount of money you raise and whether you reach your funding goal. As everything happens online, it is very easy to contribute to a project via a credit card or a payment system such as Paypal.

5 Crowdfunding makes it easier for people to try to achieve their dreams whether they want to raise money to reduce poverty or raise money to create their first music album. But how does crowdfunding actually work? First, you need to have an idea. The next stage is to describe your idea, decide how much money you want to raise, choose a deadline for your money-raising to end, and upload your project onto a crowdfunding website. Then the crowd decides—if people like your idea (and you), they will contribute money to your project. It is that simple, which is why crowdfunding has become so successful so quickly. Naturally, the better your idea is, the better chance you have of raising the money you need. The best crowdfunding marketing campaigns use text, images, videos, testimonials, and even direct communication with their potential investors. Many crowdfunding projects also provide different bonuses for different levels of funding. For example, an author raising money to publish a new book might send signed copies of the book to some funders, original artwork to others, and both to the people who contributed the most money.

6 One of the most well-known products to be funded by crowdfunding projects is the Sondors Electric Bike. This project launched on IndieGoGo on February 1, 2015 with a $75,000 goal and had raised nearly $4 million from around 7,000 people when the project closed on April 20, 2015. This represented 5,000 percent of their original goal, and demonstrated that many people wanted the product—especially as the investors could buy their bikes at a discount.

7 Another example is the Pebble watch. The first Pebble smartwatch was launched via Kickstarter in 2012. The company's funding goal was $100,000. However, after just one month, the project had raised $10,266,845 from 68,929 backers. By the end of 2014, more than one million Pebble smartwatches had been sold. In 2015, Pebble returned to Kickstarter to raise $500,000 to fund their next generation smartwatch. Within just a few weeks, the new project had raised over $18 million from more than 70,000 backers.

8 What is the future of crowdfunding? Crowdfunding has encouraged millions of people to take a direct role in international business. However, many projects do not achieve their target funding, which means that crowdfunding, like all forms of investment, is not without risk. However, successes like that of the Pebble watch show us the potential of crowdfunding, that it enables us to "create the world you want to see, one idea at a time."

NOTES

crowdfunding「クラウドファンディング」ある目的・夢・志の実現のために、不特定多数の人から資金を集める最新の資金調達方法の一つ。群衆（crowd）と財政的支援（funding）を組み合わせた造語。 **Electric Eel Shock** 日本のスリーピースバンド（主にギター、ベース、ドラムの3人で構成される最小規模のバンド）。1994年結成。1999年から約10年は海外を拠点にライブ活動を行い、国外へ向けた英語での発信も積極的に行っている。 **GoFundMe**「ゴーファンドミー」寄付ベースのクラウドファンディングを運営するサービス（インターネットサイト）。米国サンディエゴで2010年に創業。 **Kickstarter** Chapter 5のNotesを参照。 **IndieGoGo**「インディゴーゴー」世界最大の資金調達サイト（サービス）。2008年に米国サンフランシスコで誕生。Kickstarterとともに米国の２強クラウドファンディングと呼ばれる。Kickstarterがクリエイティブなプロジェクトへの資金調達を明確にしている一方、IndieGoGoは全世界のあらゆるジャンルのプロジェクトの受け皿となっている。 **Paypal**「ペイパル」オンライン決済サービス、およびそれを提供する企業名。インターネットを通じて個人および法人が送金や決済が行える。 **marketing campaign**「販売キャンペーン，販売運動」 **testimonial**「証拠，証明書」ある商品についての好意的なカスタマーレビューをその商品の広告として使う（その商品の良さを「証明」するものとして使う）手法に準ずる。そのアイデアあるいはプロジェクトがいかに優れたものか、いかに資金援助にかなうものであるか、第三者の好意的な意見などを「証拠」として使うことを指している。 **bonus**「（株主などへの）優待，特別配当金」 **Pebble watch** Chapter 5のNotesを参照。 **"create the world you want to see, one idea at a time"**「目指す世界を創ろう。ひとつずつのアイデアで」IndieGoGoのキャッチフレーズ。"one idea at a time"は"one step at a time"「一歩ずつ、一歩一歩、少しずつ」をもじったもの。

QUESTIONS FOR UNDERSTANDING

Look at the following statements. Write T if the statement is True, and F if it is False. Write the number of the paragraph where you find the answer in the parenthesis.

1. _____ According to the passage, crowdfunding is a new kind of online charity. (#   )

2. _____ Crowdfunding is similar to both borrowing money from friends and borrowing money from a bank. (#   )

3. _____ One problem with crowdfunding websites is that they keep all of the money that is raised. (#   )

4. _____ The passage indicates that how you present your idea may be more important than the idea itself. (#   )

5. _____ The passage informs us that, like traditional investing, it is possible to lose money via crowdfunding. (#   )

Chapter 13 Raising Money—The Crowdfunding Revolution

Summary

Fill each space with the best word from the list below.

| borrow | investor | contribute | launch | option | potential |

How can someone 1)_____ a new product if they do not have any money? Traditionally, people would 2)_____ money from their family or search for an 3)_____. However, because of the Internet revolution, there is now a third 4)_____ —crowdfunding. Crowdfunding allows anyone to 5)_____ money to a project simply by visiting a website. Since they began in the early 2000s, crowdfunding sites have raised billions of dollars and brought us products such as the Pebble smartwatch. The crowdfunding phenomenon shows us the 6)_____ of the Internet to change the way we do business.

Data Analysis

Use the information in the passage to complete the table using the words below.

Crowdfunding Site	Start Year	Example Project	Target Money	Actual Money Raised	Number of Backers
		Pebble smartwatch			
IndieGoGo	2008				

65

14 The Sweet Smell of Success
Using the Senses in Business

CHAPTER

GETTING READY

② 30

Choose the correct word from the list below to complete the story.

1. The Ritz Carlton hotel uses scents to _____ to people's senses for an advantage in business.

2. The hotel diffuses _____ aromas around their buildings to make the experience unique.

3. Each aroma _____ a certain reaction that makes memories more vivid and customers happier.

4. The scent also creates more _____ among customers as they come back to the hotel and are reminded of their previous enjoyable stay.

5. You can even now buy the Ritz Carlton _____ fragrance so you can experience the smell of the hotel in your own home!

| appeal | distinctive | custom | triggers | loyalty |

READING

② 31~38

1 CD 31 In the competitive environment of business, companies are always looking for new ways to attract our attention and hold our loyalty.
5 Traditionally, companies and brands have relied on appealing to the visual sense through colors, pictures, video, and text. For example, Coca-Cola has long relied on the enticing shape
10 of their bottles and their distinctive

Who can resist the smell of freshly baked bread?

66

Chapter 14 The Sweet Smell of Success—Using the Senses in Business

red and white color scheme. Likewise, who doesn't recognize the golden arches of McDonald's? A growing body of research and case studies suggests, however, that businesses should learn how to appeal to more of our senses. After all, the only way we can experience anything is through the senses.

2 ScentAir, a company established in 1994, specializes in using the senses in marketing. They argue that the sense of smell is the most under-appreciated and under-used sense in business. Yet, as ground-breaking research published in 1994 on the sense of smell by 2004 Nobel Prize winning scientists Richard Axel and Linda Buck showed, our sense of smell and our emotions are closely connected in the brain. In fact, not only do we remember a smell we have only experienced once, scents can trigger memories and emotions.

3 How have other organizations been using scents? One of the most famous examples is the airline, Singapore Airlines. They introduced their branded "Stefan Floridian Waters" scented hot towels on their flights, and customers have come to associate the airline with the scent. A Florida hospital has used scents in order to relax patients before MRI scans. After the introduction of the scents of coconut and the ocean, patient cancellations went down by 50 percent. Sony stores, Holiday Inn hotels, and many other organizations also have their own custom fragrance. In 2009, Macau introduced the largest scent system in the world at the 50,000 square meter City of Dreams casino resort. They introduced a fragrance suited to the luxury gaming resort called Rainforest, and it has been a huge success.

4 Sound should not be forgotten either. Research has shown that computer company Intel's jingle is more recognizable than their logo, for example. Golf club manufacturers such as Taylor Made and Nike have long focused heavily on the sound that their drivers make when striking the ball as this has an effect on sales. (The sense of touch is also important when it comes to golf clubs). Likewise, when you see an advertisement for a sports car, you can be sure that you will hear the sound of the engine revving so that it is easier to imagine yourself in the driver's seat. It has been shown that if you play classical music in restaurants people tend to eat more slowly and spend more money. It has also been shown that playing pop music in fast-food restaurants causes people to eat faster and leave.

5 Touch can also be useful in business. One reason that store assistants encourage customers to try on clothes is because they know that both the look and the feel are crucial to the buying decision. Likewise, a lot of the success of Apple products such as the iPhone is due to the sensory pleasure of holding them and touching them.

6 Taste is obviously at the center of the food and beverage industries. If the food you eat does not taste as nice as it looks and smells, then you probably will not try it again. Even in other industries, the sense of taste can help businesses to succeed. For example, many airlines offer similar sized seats, fly the same routes, and have similar ticket prices. So how do you choose which airline to fly? Many people will choose the one with the better taste experience. It should also be no surprise that countries famous for their cuisine such as France, Italy, China, and Thailand, are among the most visited countries in the world.

7 The idea of sensory branding is that a company should appeal to as many of the senses as possible in a consistent setting. One company that does this very well is Starbucks. The shops are immediately recognizable through their branding and design, you can smell the coffee, often more strongly outside the shop than inside, you can hear cool music playing, you can sit on the comfortable sofas and feel at home, and of course you can taste the coffee. This rich sensory environment makes you feel good, and as a result you pay more for a cup of coffee.

8 Whether you are selling or buying, it is an advantage to understand the power of our senses. As a seller, you might be able to sell more by making people happy. As a buyer, it might help you to make better buying decisions and choices. There is no doubt that the senses will continue to play a big part in business.

NOTES

Sweet Smell of Success『成功の甘き香り』1957年制作の米国映画　**Ritz Carlton**「リッツ・カールトン」100年以上の歴史をもつ世界有数の高級ホテルチェーン。　**diffuse**「(気体・液体などを)放散する」=spread　**aroma**「芳香, 香気, 香り」smellよりも強く芳しい　**custom**「オーダーメイドの, あつらえの」　**enticing**「魅惑的な」　**ScentAir**「セントエアー社」1994年設立の米国の企業。香りビジネスの業界最大手。世界105カ国に32の代理店があり、4万5,000件以上の香りマーケティングの手法をホテルやショッピングセンターなどに導入している。空間演出に香りを使うセントエアー社の手法は、1994年に米フロリダ州オークランドのディズニーワールドでアトラクションやショーの演出として使用されるようになった。　**under-**「【接頭辞】不十分に, 少なく」under-appreciated「(価値が)正当に評価されない」under-used「利用不足の」　**Stefan Floridian Waters**「ステファン・フロリディアン・ウォーターズ」シンガポール航空が独自に調合・開発したアロマ(香水)　**MRI** = magnetic resonance imaging「磁気共鳴映像法」人体に電磁波を当て、体内の原子に核磁気共鳴を起こして断層撮影を行い、得た情報をコンピューターにより画像化する生体検索手法。　**Macau**「マカオ」中国広東省にある半島。香港の対岸。1887年からポルトガル領で、1999年に中国に返還された。中国名は澳門(Aomen)。　**City of Dreams**「シティ・オ

Chapter 14 The Sweet Smell of Success—Using the Senses in Business

ブ・ドリームズ」マカオにある総合リゾート施設。2009年開業。3つの高級ホテル、ショッピングモール、カジノ、スパなどで構成される。　**Intel**「インテル」米国の大手半導体メーカー。パソコンのCPUで9割を超える市場占有率を誇る。　**Taylor Made**「テーラーメイド　ゴルフ株式会社」東京にあるゴルフ用品のメーカー。アディダス・グループ。　**Nike**「ナイキ」米国オレゴン州に本社を置くスポーツ関連商品を扱う世界的企業。社名はギリシャ神話の勝利の女神ニケ（nike）に由来する。　**revving** > rev「（エンジンなどの）回転速度を急に上げる，エンジンを始動させる」　**Apple**「アップル社，アップル　インコーポレイテッド（Apple Inc.）」米国カリフォルニア州に本社を置くデジタル家電製品・インターネット関連製品、およびこれらハードウェアに関連するソフトウェアやサービスを提供する多国籍企業。スティーブ・ジョブズ（Steve Jobs）とスティーブ・ウォズニアック（Steve Wozniak）が1976年に設立し、2007年に社名をアップル・コンピュータ（Apple Computer, Inc.）から改称した。iPhoneはアップル社の代表的な製品。　**Starbucks**「スターバックス社」1971年に米国シアトルで創業した世界的なコーヒーチェーン店。

QUESTIONS FOR UNDERSTANDING

Check the best answer for each question.

1. According to the passage, why are businesses using the five senses to appeal to us?

    a. ☐ Because they are closely connected to the emotional parts of our brains.

    b. ☐ Because the only way we experience the world is through our senses.

    c. ☐ Because Nobel Prize-winning research has shown this to be a powerful technique.

    d. ☐ Because we spend more money when our senses are stimulated.

2. Which of the following is correct about using scents in business?

    a. ☐ They can be a powerful benefit to hospitals.

    b. ☐ They are mainly used in hotels.

    c. ☐ Stefan Floridian Waters has become the standard scent for airlines.

    d. ☐ The Rainforest scent is used in Sony stores.

3. How can classical music affect our behavior in restaurants?

    a. ☐ It makes us eat faster and spend less.

    b. ☐ It makes us eat more slowly and spend less.

    c. ☐ It makes us eat faster and spend more.

    d. ☐ It makes us eat more slowly and spend more

4. According to the passage, how might people choose which airline to use?

   a. ☐ By the amount of legroom.

   b. ☐ By the price of the ticket.

   c. ☐ By the music they play.

   d. ☐ By the food they serve.

Summary

Fill each space with the best word from the list below.

| suited | revving | relied | crucial | consistent | attract |

Since the mid-1990s when some important discoveries about the sense of smell were made, this sense has been used to 1)_____ customers and then keep them. Companies who had 2)_____ on more traditional methods started to use sensory marketing with considerable success. For example, Singapore Airlines is well known for its scented hot towels. In addition, the sound of a car 3)_____ its engine is used by car manufacturers as a way to appeal to us via the sense of sound. However senses are used, it is important that they are 4)_____ to the environment and that our senses receive a 5)_____ message. In the future, businesses will find that greater knowledge of the senses will be 6)_____ for their success.

15 Online Shopping
How It Has Changed the Way We Shop

CHAPTER

GETTING READY

Choose the correct word or phrase from the list below to complete the story.

1. Singles Day was _____ by the online retailer Alibaba in 2009 as a way for people without partners to celebrate their single status.

2. It falls on November 11 each year and _____ the website Marketwatch, sales topped nine billion dollars in 2014.

3. Singles Day now has the distinction of being the biggest shopping day in the world, a day when the amount of _____ surpasses other popular shopping days such as Valentine's Day and other traditional holiday periods.

4. _____ and founder of Alibaba, Jack Ma, said he was most worried about being able to complete the deliveries on time—some 260 million of them.

5. Ma _____ that Singles Day will become a global holiday by 2020.

| invented | predicts | entrepreneur | purchases | according to |

READING

1 English entrepreneur Michael Aldrich invented online shopping in 1979, and it is now over 20 years since the first online purchase. According to *The Daily Telegraph* newspaper the item was Sting's *Ten Summoner's Tales*, a popular music album released in 1993. This was the time that many famous online businesses began. eBay and Amazon were both launched in 1995. Google was launched in 1998, and in 2000 they released Adwords, the world's most

5

widely used online advertising service. The year 1998 also saw the launch of Paypal, a service that made online shopping with credit cards safe and
5 secure. Alibaba, now the largest online shop in the world, was launched in 2003. In less than ten years, online shopping became an everyday activity. A recent survey in Britain showed
10 that 95 percent of people shop online. In 2014, British shoppers spent over 100 billion pounds online.

A computer and a credit card are all you need to start shopping.

2 🎵 The success of online shopping has been driven by convenience. For example, Amazon's Japanese site, amazon.co.jp, offers customers more than 100 million items. People can access online stores 24 hours a day and items that are
15 ordered will usually be delivered within a few days. People can avoid queueing and the stress of driving to a shop and parking. Because online retailers do not maintain traditional shops and shop staff, they can offer many products at a lower price. These savings mean that many online stores offer free delivery.

3 🎵 The Internet has changed shopping in other ways. When buying goods
20 and services before the Internet, customers might rely on the expertise of shop staff and would perhaps compare the prices offered by a few shops or service providers. The Internet allows us to quickly compare products and prices, and to see how satisfied other customers are by reading online reviews. There are even websites that provide rankings of goods and services. Some online stores such
25 as Amazon use information about what we have bought in the past to present us with advertisements for other products. The practice of "showrooming" has also developed. This is when people visit a shop to check the actual product in real life before buying it, usually online for a cheaper price.

4 🎵 When online shopping became popular, many people predicted that
30 traditional shops would disappear. A quick visit to any high street shows that this has not been the case. Many large stores have simply added online shopping to their main "bricks and mortar" business. For example, most of the major supermarkets in Britain, including Asda and Tesco, offer online services, as do supermarket chains like AEON in Japan.

Chapter 15 Online Shopping—How It Has Changed the Way We Shop

5 However, while online shopping is convenient, it cannot replace the experience of going out shopping. As a result, instead of disappearing, high streets and malls have made shopping a more appealing experience by offering attractive places to eat, child care, and events. For people who do not want to wait at home for a delivery, some stores allow you to order online and then pick the item up the next day from a local shop. When the British retailer, John Lewis, began this service in 2011, it rapidly became popular, and in 2015, 56 percent of online shoppers used this service.

6 A recent trend has been the growth of shopping on smartphones and tablets. In 2014, more than half of British online sales took place via mobile phones. The portability of smartphones and tablets is making the distinction between online and offline shopping less clear. Shops can use your location information and send you targeted advertisements and directions to nearby shops, something which has boosted sales for the Adidas sports brand.

7 There is no question that online shopping is here to stay. Retailers around the world continue to search for new ways to exploit the Internet. However, it can be argued that what people want from a shopping experience is very limited. They want competitive prices, value, convenience, a good selection of products, and they want to enjoy the shopping process. Whether online or offline, the retailers that meet these needs will continue to be successful.

NOTES

Singles Day「光棍節（こうこんせつ）」中国で主に若者たちが11月11日に祝う「独身者の日」　**Alibaba**「アリババ社」阿里巴巴集団 (Alibaba Group)。中国の電子商取引最大手。創業者のジャック・マーは元英語教師で、アリババ社を1999年に設立した。アジア最大のECサイト (electronic commerce site=インターネット上で商品を販売するウェブサイト) を運営するほか、製造業者と仕入れ業者の取引の場を提供する世界規模の企業間電子商取引サービスを展開。　**fall on**「（日付が）〜に当たる」　**Marketwatch**「マーケットウォッチ」主に企業の経営者層や個人投資家に向けてビジネス・経済に関連するニュースを配信する金融情報ウェブサイト　**Jack Ma**「ジャック・マー（馬雲）」アリババ社の創業者、元CEO。現在、経営執行役会長。　***The Daily Telegraph***「デイリー・テレグラフ紙」英国ロンドンに本拠地のあるテレグラフ・メディア・グループ社 (Telegraph Media group) が発行する日刊紙。1855年創刊。高級紙として知られ、また英国の一般紙サイズの新聞では発行部数1位である。　**Sting**「スティング」英国のミュージシャン(1951-)。*Ten Summoner's Tales* はスティングの5枚目のソロアルバム。1993年発売。　**eBay**「イーベイ」インターネットオークションを中心としたサービスを提供するウェブサイト。またはそのサイトを運営する米国の企業eBay Inc.のこと。　**Amazon**「アマゾン」米国Amazon.com社が運営する世界最大級のインターネット通販サイト。1994年創業、95年にネット上でのサービス開始。　**Adwords**「アドワーズ」検索エンジンGoogleを運営するグーグル社が広告主に提供しているサービス。Google検索結果に連動して画面上にウェブ広告を掲載する。Googleの利用者が、広告主があらかじめ登録したキーワードに近い言葉で検索を行った際に、広告が検索結果と同時に画面に表示される。掲載自体にはコストがかからず、その広告が実際にクリックされた回数分のみ

費用が発生するPPC（ペイ・パー・クリック＝クリック課金型のインターネット広告）。　**Paypal**「ペイパル」オンライン決済サービス（Chapter 13のNotesの参照）。1998年にeBayの支払いシステムとして始まった。　**retailer**「小売業者」　**high street**「目抜き通り」　**"bricks and mortar" business**「（オンライン店舗を持たない）実店舗だけの商売、従来方式の小売りビジネス、昔ながらのビジネス」直訳は「れんがとモルタル（セメント）の」（ビルで行う）ビジネス。　**Asda**「アズダ」英国流通最大手の一つ。米国ウォルマートグループに属す。　**Tesco**「テスコ」英国最大手、世界でも三本の指に入る小売業者。　**AEON**「イオン」イオン株式会社。日本の大手の小売業者。国内外140余の企業で構成されるイオングループの統括企業。　**John Lewis**「ジョン・ルイス」英国の百貨店チェーン。　**[be] here to stay**「普及している，定着する」

QUESTIONS FOR UNDERSTANDING

Look at the following statements. Write T if the statement is True, and F if it is False. Write the number of the paragraph where you find the answer in the parenthesis.

1. _____ The first online purchase triggered a series of technological developments in online shopping.　(#　　)

2. _____ When we shop online, we tend to rely on the opinion of many people about a purchase, rather than just one person.　(#　　)

3. _____ "Showrooming" is when you look at the physical product in a store and then go to a computer and order it online.　(#　　)

4. _____ People still love going to real shops and malls for their shopping experiences.　(#　　)

5. _____ The distinction between online and offline shopping remains very clear.　(#　　)

Chapter 15 Online Shopping—How It Has Changed the Way We Shop

Summary

Fill each space with the best word from the list below.

launched	replace	predicted	retailers	process	allowed

Since the mid-1990s when the first online purchase was made, online shopping has become a phenomenal success. Major online shops Amazon and eBay were 1)_____ in 1995, and billions of dollars are now spent online on a daily basis around the world. Many 2)_____ have been quick to add an online shop to their existing operations to maximize sales. The Internet has 3)_____ people to browse thousands of items easily and quickly. They can also obtain recommendations and information about the products via online reviews. Online shopping has become so successful that many 4)_____ that it would 5)_____ traditional high streets and malls. This has not been the case. It seems that people still love the 6)_____ of shopping, whether online or off.

Data Analysis

Use the information in the passage to complete the timeline about online shopping.

1979	1994	1995	1998	2000	2003	2011	2014
		Amazon and eBay launched			Alibaba founded		

Chapter 16

Tesla and the Electric Car
The New Age of Electric Automobiles

Getting Ready

Choose the correct word or phrase from the list below to complete the story.

1. In our world, automobiles are so _____ that we rarely think about how they work.

2. Automobiles are powered by engines called internal _____ engines.

3. These engines burn _____ such as gasoline and diesel inside small pistons to create power.

4. The _____ genius of the automobile engine is in how it converts the up-and-down motion of the pistons to the circular motion of the wheels.

5. However, the success of the internal combustion engine might result in its disappearance because the _____ from the burnt fossil fuels are damaging the environment.

| commonplace | fundamental | emissions | fossil fuels | combustion |

Reading

1 Electric cars are finally becoming commonplace on roads around the world. Major car brands such as Nissan, BMW, Toyota, Volkswagen, and Ford are now mass-producing electric cars. The Nissan Leaf is currently the world's top-selling electric car, with over 75,000 cars sold in the United States by March 2015. In addition, many governments are actively supporting this automotive revolution as concerns about protecting the environment and fuel efficiency grow among the people of many countries.

Chapter 16   Tesla and the Electric Car—The New Age of Electric Automobiles

2 Interestingly, electric cars have been around for a long time. The first electric cars went on sale in 1884 and were designed by the British engineer Thomas Parker. His interest in electric cars stemmed from concerns about the smoke and pollution in London at the time. It is interesting to note that worries about the environment remain as relevant as ever nearly 150 years later. At the beginning of the 20th century, 40 percent of automobiles in the United States were powered by steam, 38 percent by electricity, and 22 percent by gasoline. By the time of the Second World War, though, both steam and electric cars had almost disappeared because they could not compete with the power and efficiency of the internal combustion engine developed by Karl Benz and Gottlieb Daimler.

3 Why has the electric car returned now? Perhaps the main reasons are connected to our use of fossil fuels such as gasoline. It is well-known that using these fuels can cause damage to the environment. As a result, governments began to issue requirements for zero-emission cars to be produced. For example, in 1990 the California Air Resources Board announced that all car companies must produce at least two percent of their cars as zero-emissions cars by 1998. It is also well-known that fossil fuels will one day run out. As a result, when oil prices rise, so does interest in electric cars. Perhaps a more fundamental reason why electric cars are returning to our roads now is that electric car technology is finally able to compete with the internal combustion engine. In 1997 Toyota helped to pave the way with its Prius hybrid car, combining a gasoline engine with a rechargeable electric motor. This changed people's minds about electric car technology and made it easier to fully embrace electric cars. In addition, electric cars cost less to run per year. One estimate is that electric cars cost around 75 percent less to run than traditional gasoline cars.

4 What are the drawbacks with electric cars? It seems that many of the problems associated with electric cars have been eliminated. Batteries now hold their charge longer, and the best electric cars can travel over 120km before needing to recharge. This is accompanied by much better infrastructure for electric cars. In March 2015, the U.S. Department of Energy stated that there were over 9,000 charging stations and over 21,000 charging outlets in the United States. However, electric cars currently cost more to buy than their gasoline counterparts. The Nissan Leaf, for example, costs $29,000 whereas a comparable gasoline car such as the Versa-Note costs only around $14,000.

5 No discussion of the electric car is complete without the mention of the Tesla Company. Named after the legendary inventor Nikola Tesla and founded by Elon Musk, the company has come to represent a new kind of electric car. The Tesla Model S has become an iconic product of its time, featuring highly advanced battery technology and a touch screen display for the driver. By far the most attractive and sporty of all the electric cars on the market, it can reach 100 km/h in 3.8 seconds and can travel over 500km between charges. Tesla also constantly improves its cars with software updates. For example, a recent update made it easier for drivers to judge how far their vehicle can travel. The ability to update software in this way is unique to Tesla and a glimpse of the future of transportation. However, a Model S costs over $65,000 and is in such high demand that there is a months-long waiting list.

6 Whether you buy a Nissan Leaf or a Tesla Model S, it seems that, after a false start in the 1880s, the electric car is here to stay and will bring considerable benefits both for the consumer and the environment.

The Tesla Model S – the fastest and most technologically advanced production electric car.

NOTES

electric car「電気自動車」　**internal combustion engine**「内燃機関，内燃エンジン」　**fossil fuel**「化石燃料」　**genius** [the〜]「神髄，特質」　**result in 〜**「〜という結果になる」　**emission**「排出，放出」　**commonplace**「ごく普通の，平凡な」　**mass-produce**「大量生産する」　**Nissan Leaf**「日産リーフ」世界初の量産型電気自動車。2010年12月から日本・米国で販売開始。2011年欧州カー・オブ・ザ・イアー、2011年ワールド・カー・オブ・ザ・イヤーなどを獲得。**have been around**「（業界で）（〜年の）歴史がある，存在している」　**Thomas Parker**「トマス・パーカー(1843-1915)」英国の技術者・発明家。公共用・家庭用の電気システムを整備し、電気で走るトラム（路面電車）の開発に携わる。「英国のエジソン」と呼ばれたこともある。**Karl Benz**「カール・フリードリヒ・ベンツ(1844-1929)」ドイツのエンジン設計者・自動車技術者。妻とともに自動車メーカーのメルセデス・ベンツの礎を築いた。**Gottlieb Daimler**「ゴットリープ・ダイムラー(1834-1900)」ドイツの機械技術者・自動車生産者。四輪自動車の原型を生み出した。最初の高速内燃機関を生産し、ガソリン自動車の製作に成功した。ダイムラー自動車会社を設立した。**zero-emission car**「排ガスを出さない車，無公害車」　**California Air Resources Board**「カリフォルニア大気資源委員会（CARB）」　**run out**「尽きる，枯渇する」　**pave the way**「道を開く」　**Prius**「プリウス」トヨタ自動車から発売された世界初の量産型ハイブリッド・カー　**counterpart**「対応するもの，対の片方」　**Versa-Note**「ヴァーサノート」日本名は

Chapter 16 Tesla and the Electric Car—The New Age of Electric Automobiles

「ノート」。日産の自動車。　**Tesla Company**「テスラ社」正式名称は「テスタモーターズ」（Tesla Motors）。「電気自動車がガソリン車を超えられることを証明したいと願った」（同社公式ウェブサイトから）米国シリコンバレーの技術者たちによって2003年に設立された。電気自動車の開発と販売を行う。社名の由来はNikola Teslaから。　**Nikola Tesla**「ニコラ・テスラ(1856-1943)」クロアチア生まれの米国の電気工学者・発明家。1884年に渡米し、エジソン研究所に勤務、その後独立した。高圧交流発電に成功し、大電力の輸送技術の基礎を確立した。　**Elon Musk**「イーロン・マスク(1971-)」南ア出身の米国の企業家　**here to stay** 15章のNotesを参照

QUESTIONS FOR UNDERSTANDING

Check the best answer for each question.

1. According to information presented in the passage, which of the following sentences about the Nissan Leaf is correct?
    a. ☐ The Nissan Leaf is being mass-produced by Nissan, BMW, Volkswagen, Toyota, and Ford.
    b. ☐ More than 75,000 Nissan Leaf cars have been sold worldwide.
    c. ☐ The Nissan Leaf became available in the United States in March 2015.
    d. ☐ The Nissan Leaf is being mass-produced by many governments.

2. According to the passage, what are two reasons why electric cars are becoming popular?
    a. ☐ Fossil fuels are in good supply and electric car technology has improved.
    b. ☐ Fossil fuels are running out and electric car technology has improved.
    c. ☐ Fossil fuels are in good supply but electric car technology has not improved.
    d. ☐ Fossil fuels are running out but electric car technology has not improved.

3. According to the passage, which of the following is **not** a drawback of electric cars?
    a. ☐ Electric cars cost 75 percent less to run than gasoline cars.
    b. ☐ Electric cars are much more expensive than gasoline cars.
    c. ☐ Electric cars run out of power much faster than gasoline cars.
    d. ☐ Electric cars have far fewer places to refuel than gasoline cars.

4. According to the passage, what is special about Tesla electric cars?
   a. ☐ They are the most beautiful electric cars.
   b. ☐ They are the fastest electric cars.
   c. ☐ They have regular software updates.
   d. ☐ All of the above.

Summary

Fill each space with the best word or phrase from the list below.

| counterparts | charge | embrace | run out | compete with | drawbacks |

Humanity fell in love with cars in the 20th century, but in the 21st century we are discovering the 1)_____ of the internal combustion engine. As fossil fuels look likely to 2)_____ in the near future, perhaps it is time to 3)_____ the electric car. However, while electric cars are much less polluting than their gasoline-powered 4)_____, they are far from perfect. Until an electric car can travel as far on a single 5)_____ as a gasoline car can with a full tank of fuel, electric cars will not be able to seriously 6)_____ traditional cars.

CHAPTER 17

The Midas Touch
Can You Have Too Much Money?

GETTING READY

② 57

Choose the correct word or phrase from the list below to complete the story.

1. When we say someone has "the Midas touch" we mean that they are much more successful than _____. But who was Midas? Midas was an ancient Greek king, and this is his story.

2. King Midas loved gold, but no matter how much _____ he had, he was not satisfied. One day, the god Dionysus gave Midas the ability to turn whatever he touched into gold.

3. At first Midas was pleased, but he soon discovered that this gift was really a(n) _____.

4. Everything he touched turned into gold—including his food and drink. As a result, King Midas realized that he was _____ die because of his love of gold. Eventually, Dionysus took away Midas's golden touch and Midas lived a simple life after that.

5. So when we hear the expression, "the Midas touch," we should celebrate a person's achievements, but also remember that the _____ for success always has a cost.

| likely to | average | struggle | curse | wealth |

READING

② 58~63

1 What does being rich mean to you? Does it mean owning penthouse condos in Roppongi and Hawaii, or eating gold-plated sushi? If they think hard about it, most people have similar ideas of what being rich means. They mostly want two things: security and freedom. Security means that they don't have to

81

worry about paying bills or buying the things they need or want. Freedom means that they don't need to work and can enjoy life. Being rich sounds great, but is it possible to have too much money?

How much money is too much?

2 How much money do you have with you today? Does the person next to you have more or less? It is unlikely that they have the same amount of money. In other words, the wealth in your classroom is distributed unequally—some people have more, and some people have less. This is true all over the world. How unequal is the distribution of the world's wealth today? Globally, the richest one percent of people own about 35 percent of the world's wealth. In fact, in 2014 just 65 people had more wealth than the world's poorest *3.5 billion* people.

3 Over the last 50 years, global inequality has generally fallen. However, in some countries, including Russia, the United States, and Britain, it has increased. For example, in Japan, the average company CEO earns about 65 times the salary of the lowest paid worker. In Norway, the ratio is 58:1, and in Sweden, it is 89:1. In the United States, the ratio is 354:1.

4 But is this wealth inequality a bad thing? The U.S. and U.K. governments say that the rich should pay less tax because they create jobs and help to develop the economy. If this is true, then having rich people benefits the population of a country and makes everyone richer. Unfortunately, research over many years shows that it is not true. Firstly, about 65 percent of wealthy people inherited some or all of their money. Secondly, paying people very high salaries and bonuses actually reduces the number of jobs in a country. For example, in 2013, Lloyds Bank in Britain paid bonuses of £365 million to its top 2,000 employees (an average of £182,500 each), with the top five employees getting bonuses of more than £1 million each. The national average salary in Britain is £27,000, which means that £365 million is enough money to employ 13,500 people for one year. Furthermore, the 2008 Great Recession was caused by rich people trying to make more money. The result was that millions of people around the world lost their jobs and became poorer while the rich got even richer. This negative

Chapter 17   The Midas Touch—Can You Have Too Much Money?

impact was not limited to the 2008 Great Recession, however. In 2014, the OECD reported that even though the richest people had become much richer, growing wealth inequality between 1985 and 2005 had actually *slowed* the growth of the global economy by between five and ten percent.

5 To add insult to injury, being rich doesn't even make you happy. The struggles of young people who are cursed with great wealth are easy to find in literature and in the media. In fact, the famously ironic expression, "Poor little rich girl," was from the title of a 1917 movie. While wealth can be a curse, poverty is worse. Poor people have worse health, education, and living conditions. They are more likely to suffer from disease, mental illness, abuse, crime, and violence. They are more likely to kill themselves or be murdered. It should be no surprise that the happiest countries in the world are the ones with the lowest inequality.

6 Is there a solution to the problem of wealth inequality? The simplest is to increase the tax paid by the wealthy. The taxes taken by the government are used to develop the country's infrastructure and education, which means that the average wealth of the country goes up. This is the model used in Scandinavia and Japan. Today, even some of the wealthiest people, such as U.S. investor Warren Buffet, say they pay too little tax compared to poorer people. The French Revolution in 1789 and the Russian Revolution in 1917, which cost millions of lives, show us what can happen if we do not increase the taxes paid by the rich. Reducing wealth inequality is literally a matter of life and death.

NOTES

Midas touch「(the ~) 何でも金にしてしまう能力，金もうけの才能」　**Midas**「ミダス」ギリシア神話に登場する小アジアのフリギアの王　**Dionysus**「ディオニュソス」ギリシア神話で酒と演劇と多産の神。ローマ神話のバッカス (Bacchus) にあたる。　**penthouse**「最上階の高級アパート」　**condo**=condominium「分譲マンション[アパート]」　**CEO**=chief executive officer「最高経営責任者」　**Lloyds Bank**「ロイズ銀行」英国の大手商業銀行　**the 2008 Great Recession** 2008年に起きた世界的金融危機、いわゆる「リーマン・ショック」(Lehman Shockは和製英語) のこと。米国の投資銀行リーマン・ブラザーズの破綻に端を発したため、日本ではこのように呼ばれる。　**OECD**=Organization for Economic Cooperation and Development「経済協力開発機構」1961年に発足した先進工業国中心の国際経済協力機構。経済成長、発展途上国援助、通商拡大の3つを主要目的とする。　**add insult to injury**「ひどい目に遭わせた上に侮辱を加える，さらに追い打ちをかける，踏んだり蹴ったりの目に遭わせる」　**Poor little rich girl** メアリー・ピックフォード主演の米映画のタイトルは『The Poor Little Rich Girl』(1917)　**Warren Buffet**「ウォーレン・バフェット」米国の投資家・慈善事業家。世界最大の投資持株会社バークシャー・ハサウェイの筆頭株主で会長兼CEO。

Questions for Understanding

Look at the following statements. Write T if the statement is True, and F if it is False. Write the number of the paragraph where you find the answer in the parenthesis.

1. _____ According to the passage, 65 people own half of the world's wealth. (#)

2. _____ Wealth inequality has increased, except in Russia, the United States, and Britain. (#)

3. _____ The more rich people there are in a country, the richer everyone becomes. (#)

4. _____ The bonuses paid to some Lloyd's Bank staff in 2013 were the same as an average worker would earn in about 40 years. (#)

5. _____ According to the passage, wealthier people are less likely to be affected by crime and violence than poor people. (#)

Summary

Fill each space with the best word from the list below.

| inherit   security   reduce   benefit   inequality   unlikely |

If someone offered you a fortune, it is 1)_____ that you would refuse. Wealth can give us the 2)_____ to live our lives free from worry and fear. However, it is becoming clear that society does not 3)_____ when there are too many rich people. If 4)_____ is too high in a society, it can 5)_____ the ability of the majority to become richer. One way to stop this from happening is to cut how much money rich people can 6)_____ from their parents through taxes.

Chapter 17 The Midas Touch—Can You Have Too Much Money?

DATA ANALYSIS

Use the information in the passage to complete the chart below.

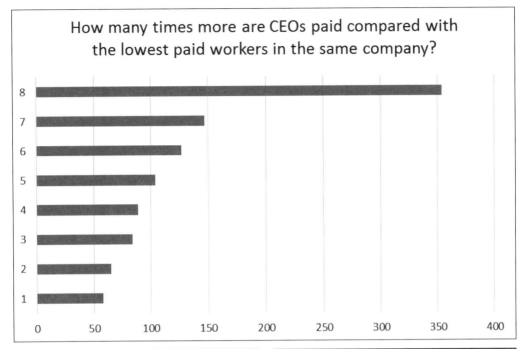

How many times more are CEOs paid compared with the lowest paid workers in the same company?

1		
2		
3	Britain	85:1
4		

5	France	104:1
6	Spain	127:1
7	Germany	147:1
8		

CHAPTER 18

The Hidden Crime
Modern Slavery

GETTING READY   ② 65

Choose the correct word from the list below to complete the story.

1. In 2012, two Chinese workers were _____ from a factory in Ishikawa Prefecture by a Japanese lawyer.

2. They had been _____ to work 16 hours a day, six days a week, with only a 15-minute lunch break. They were only paid 400 yen per hour for their work, instead of 691 yen per hour.

3. They complained to their boss, but he _____ them and took their passports away.

4. It is _____ that there are nearly 155,000 foreign interns in Japan, mostly from China.

5. Although treating foreign interns differently to Japanese staff is _____, a 2012 survey found that nearly 80 percent of companies with foreign interns broke the law.

| ignored | estimated | rescued | forced | outlawed |

READING   ② 66~75

1 🅲🅳 66 What do you think of when you hear the word slavery? Perhaps you think of Roman gladiators or the Africans kidnapped from their homes and shipped to America. Whatever the idea of slavery makes you think of, however, it is not likely that you will think of people being slaves in the 21st century.

5   **2** 🅲🅳 67 No one knows how many people have experienced slavery through history, but the number is certainly in the tens of millions. Nearly every civilization kept slaves at some time. In many cultures, from Asia to the Americas, the

losers of a war became the slaves of the winners. In a small number of these cultures, such as ancient Rome, it was possible for a slave to become a free citizen. However, most slaves could not expect to experience freedom after their enslavement and died as slaves.

What can YOU do to help end slavery?

3 However, during the 19th century, governments began to be convinced that slavery was wrong, and it was gradually outlawed. International agreements banning slavery were signed in 1926 and 1930, although these were ignored by some countries during World War II. In 1956, the United Nations Supplementary Convention on the Abolition of Slavery, the Slave Trade, and Institutions and Practices Similar to Slavery made all forms of slavery a crime. Many people felt that slavery would finally become a thing of the past.

4 But they would be wrong. In 2013, the Global Slavery Index estimated that at least 25 million people were living as slaves around the world, including 10 million children. It is estimated that about 14 million people are held in slavery in India, nearly three million in China, two million in Pakistan, and nearly a million in Nigeria. Slaves are also held in Ethiopia, Russia, Thailand, and nearly every other country in smaller numbers.

5 Modern slaves are not sold in markets: 21st century slavery comes in many different forms. One of the most common is debt bondage. Debt bondage starts when someone borrows some money at a very high interest rate. Soon the debt becomes too big to ever be paid back, and instead the lender forces the debtor to work for free until the debt is paid. But the debt can never be paid, so the slavery lasts a lifetime. Sometimes the rest of the slave's family is also enslaved to pay off the impossible debt.

6 In 2009, the British police found a 20-year-old woman in the street. The woman was deaf and could not speak English. In order to hear her story, the police needed to teach her sign language. When she was 10 years old, she had been taken from her parents to pay a debt. She had been smuggled into England by her "owners" and forced to cook for them and clean their house. She had no free time, never left the house, and had to sleep in the cellar. In 2012, the couple that had kept her as a slave were sent to prison.

7 Another common form of slavery is forced marriage. This occurs when young women and girls are forced to get married, often by their own families. Once married, these women often find it extremely difficult to escape their husbands and are at a very high risk of mistreatment, violence, and death.

8 In August 2012, a Slovakian woman working in Hungary was kidnapped. She was taken to England and forced to marry a man from Pakistan. The Pakistani man needed to marry a woman from the E.U. so that he could get a visa to continue living in England. The woman was kept locked in his house and often beaten. The police rescued her in October 2012.

9 Finally, there is forced labor. This often happens when criminal gangs offer people jobs in a foreign country that sound good but are actually fake. Instead, they have their passports taken away and are forced to work for little or no pay. Nepalese workers working in Qatar to prepare for the 2022 Soccer World Cup had to live in filthy accommodation and were forced to work for 12 hours a day, seven days a week. Furthermore, they were not paid for months, and were sent home – without pay – if they complained. In 2012, more than 1,000 Nepalese workers were hospitalized due to falls and other accidents, and between the beginning of June 2013 and the start of August 2013, more than 40 Nepalese workers died.

10 Slavery was an important part of human civilization for thousands of years before people realized that it is a crime against humanity. Too many people think that slavery is a thing of the past, but the truth is that today, there are still millions of slaves suffering around the world. We must not rest until the last slave is returned to freedom.

NOTES

slavery「奴隷制」 **intern**「実習生, 医学研修生」 **it is estimated that ~** Chapter 4のNotesを参照 **outlaw**「禁止する, 非合法化する」 **gladiator**「(古代ローマの)剣闘士」 **Supplementary Convention on the Abolition of Slavery, the Salve Trade, and Institutions and Practices Similar to Slavery**「奴隷制度、奴隷取引並びに奴隷制度類似の制度及び慣行の廃止に関する補足条約」国際連合が国際連盟による奴隷条約（1926年）を継承し、さらに債務奴隷や農奴、自由な意志に反した結婚、児童労働を含む奴隷全般とそれに類する制度や風習、奴隷貿易を禁止するための条約。1956年採択、翌57年発効。日本は未批准。 **Global Slavery Index**「世界奴隷指数」オーストラリアのウォークフリー財団(Walk Free Foundation)が2013年から発表している、世界で奴隷状態に置かれている人々の数データ。 **debt bondage**「借金による束縛」 **enslave**「奴隷にする」 **smuggle**「密入（出）国させる」 **forced marriage**「強制結婚」 **forced labor**「強制労働」 **Nepalese**「ネパール（人・語）の」 **Qatar**「カタール」アラビア半島東部の首長国

Chapter 18   The Hidden Crime—Modern Slavery

QUESTIONS FOR UNDERSTANDING

Check the best answer for each question.

1. Which of the following statements about slavery is correct?

    a. ☐ Slavery was not common among ancient civilizations.

    b. ☐ Most slaves became free after a short time.

    c. ☐ It was rare for slaves to become free.

    d. ☐ Many slaves were taken from America to Africa.

2. What is debt bondage?

    a. ☐ A person is forced to work because they cannot pay back money they borrowed.

    b. ☐ A person promises to work because they cannot pay back money they borrowed.

    c. ☐ A person is made to marry someone they don't want to marry.

    d. ☐ A person is offered a good overseas job, but is then forced to do a different job.

3. Which of the following is a kind of modern slavery?

    a. ☐ People are sold in markets as slaves.

    b. ☐ People are made into slaves after a war.

    c. ☐ People are tricked into slavery.

    d. ☐ None of the above.

4. What is the similarity between ancient and modern slavery?

    a. ☐ Slaves can become free if they work hard.

    b. ☐ Slaves can be found in many countries.

    c. ☐ Most slaves are in India.

    d. ☐ None of the above.

Summary

Fill each space with the best word from the list below.

> debt criminal millions slavery force rescue

Although it became illegal, 1)_____ did not end. Today, 2)_____ gangs all around the world make 3)_____ of people work for little or no pay. Other people become slaves because they can't pay a 4)_____, or because their families 5)_____ them into a marriage they don't want. We cannot ignore the suffering of these people and must do all we can to 6)_____ them from their bondage.

19 Someone Is Watching Me
Cyber-spies and Cyber-warfare

CHAPTER

GETTING READY

Choose the correct word or phrase from the list below to complete the story.

1. TOR is free software that can help to protect people from unwanted _____.

2. TOR stands for The Onion Router and it uses multiple levels of encryption so that our Internet activity may not be _____ by outsiders.

3. The first version of the software _____ 2002, when some computer scientists presented it at the 13th USENIX Security Symposium.

4. It is said that TOR's security systems cannot be _____ by even the best hackers.

5. It is _____ that over 2.5 million people around the world use TOR every day.

| estimated | surveillance | defeated | dates from | monitored |

READING

1 An extraordinary range of our daily activities are connected to the Internet via computers and other devices. These networks often contain information that has a very high value to criminals such as identity-related data, credit card numbers, bank account details, medical records, and even state secrets. As a result, there is a kind of technological war going on which is being fought between those trying to protect data and computer

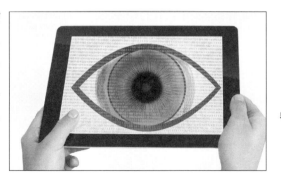
Is your computer spying on you?

networks and those who are trying to steal from them or manipulate them. Symantec, a company which develops anti-virus protection software, publishes the Internet Security Threat Report every year. According to the 2014 report over 552 million identities were illegally exposed in 2013; there was a 91 percent
⁵ increase in targeted attacks; and the number of security breaches increased by 62 percent. Norton, a computer security company, estimates that the annual cost of cybercrime is at least $100 billion.

2 🎧 79 Cyber-attacks can be devastating. In June 2010, a kind of computer virus, known as a worm, called Stuxnet, was successfully inserted into the computer
¹⁰ network that controlled the Iranian nuclear fuel processing systems. At least 20 percent of the equipment in the infected nuclear facilities was destroyed, and the Iranian nuclear research program was put back years. It is widely believed that a government spy agency created the Stuxnet worm specifically to target the nuclear program. The most widespread worm in history, Conficker,
¹⁵ has so far infected between 9 and 15 million Windows computers in more than 190 countries around the world, including those of the French Navy, the U.K. Ministry of Defence, the German Army, and the Norwegian police. First detected in 2008, the purpose of this worm is to create a network of slave computers called a botnet that can then be controlled by the worm's creators. Although
²⁰ many government computers have been infected, the creators are not spies and actually use the botnets to send spam. Microsoft has offered a $250,000 reward for information about who created the worm.

3 🎧 80 Computer networks started becoming widespread in the 1980s, and the earliest cyber-attacks date from that time. The first acknowledged case of a
²⁵ cyber-attack was in 1986 and was called "Cuckoo's Egg." It was carried out on an American military network by some German computer scientists working for the intelligence service of the Soviet Union, the KGB. Other attacks followed, although they are not widely known, including Moonlight Maze, Solar Sunrise, Titan Rain, and Byzantine Hades. The introduction of the Internet in the 1990s
³⁰ accelerated the level of connectivity and the possibility of more attacks. These days air traffic control systems, stock markets, power stations, cars, and even refrigerators are connected to the Internet and potentially vulnerable. Indeed, early in 2015, the U.K. and the U.S. governments agreed to join forces to combat the real threat posed by cyber-warfare after a suspected attack by North Korea.

Chapter 19 Someone Is Watching Me—Cyber-spies and Cyber-warfare

As the use of mobile devices, wearable technology and medical devices such as implants, which can all connect to the Internet become more common, the range of targets and risks will increase.

4 Cyber-spying is also a concern. Especially since the 9/11 attacks, governments around the world and in particular the U.S. government have been concerned with monitoring all kinds of electronic traffic in order to detect terrorist threats. The NSA, a U.S. government surveillance agency, has taken the ability to spy to a new level with programs such as ECHELON, originally created during the Cold War, which allows for the live monitoring and storage of e-mail, phone, fax, and other data. There is also the PRISM (2007) program, which allows tracking of activity across major search and social media sites such as Google and Facebook. The now famous whistleblower, Edward Snowden, exposed the full extent of the PRISM program when he revealed that the U.S. and U.K. governments had been routinely breaking the law by illegally accessing information without a warrant.

5 What can we do to protect ourselves from attacks and spying? The only surefire defense from attacks and spying is to disconnect completely from the Internet. However, apart from being impractical, most of us would not trade the loss of convenience for total safety from attack. Instead, we can use anti-virus protection and encryption software. We can also use common sense and avoid using the Internet to transmit certain kinds of sensitive information such as passwords and credit card numbers. However, whatever we do may not be enough. A recent article in *The Guardian* reported that the U.S. and U.K. governments have already defeated most Internet privacy and security systems.

6 While the Internet has brought convenience, it has brought dangers, too. With a computer and an Internet connection, it is now possible to launch cyber-attacks on governments, institutions, companies, and individuals. Not only that, governments can turn this technology on their own citizens to spy on them and infringe their right to privacy. The actions of Edward Snowden have gone a long way to show us the extent of the problem, but it will not be easy to fix. It looks like cyber-warfare and cyber-spying are set to become part of everyone's life.

NOTES

Someone is watching me 英小説家ジョージ・オーウェルの未来小説『1984』(1949)での有名なフレーズ "Big brother is watching you"（ビッグ・ブラザーがあなたを見守っている）のもじり。『1984』では全体主義国家における監視社会が描かれており、このフレーズはしばしば「政府や権力者が人々を監視している」の意で使われる。　**TOR**=The Onion Router「トーア，トール」インターネット上で通信経路の特定を困難にすることで、匿名での通信を行う技術。あるいはそうした技術を実現するためのソフトウェア。名称はタマネギの皮のように何重にも暗号化技術を重ねることに由来する。　**encryption**「（情報の）暗号化」　**USENIX Security Symposium** 1988年にUNIX Security Workshopとして始まり、1995年に現在の名称となった。実用的なコンピューターセキュリティー・ネットワークセキュリティー技術に関して、世界で最も注目されている国際会議の一つ。　**via** Chapter 6のNotesを参照。　**Symantec**「シマンテック」セキュリティー、ストレージ、システム管理ソリューションを提供する世界有数の米ソフトウェア企業。1982年に当時の最先端の技術を持つ複数のコンピューター科学者によって設立され、その後50カ国に1万8,500人の従業員を擁するまでに成長した。Internet Security Threat Report（インターネットセキュリティー脅威レポート）などを発行。　**security breach**「セキュリティー違反，安全への侵害」　**worm**「ワーム」= computer worm「コンピューターワーム」悪意のあるプログラム（マルウェア）の一種。ユーザーに気付かれないようにコンピューターに侵入し、破壊活動などを行う。ウイルスと異なり、宿主となるファイルやプログラムを必要としない。　**slave computer**「スレーブコンピューター，従計算機」　**botnet**「ボットネット」多くのパソコンやサーバーに攻撃用プログラム（ボット）を送り込み、外部から遠隔操作で一斉に攻撃を行わせるネットワークのこと。　**KGB**「（旧ソ連の）国家保安委員会」1954～1991年に反体制派の取り締まり、国境警備、海外での情報収集などを行った。　**NSA**=National Security Agency「（米国の）国家安全保障局」国防総省に所属し、世界各地で通信傍受に当たる。　**ECHELON**「エシュロン」英米を中心に運営しているといわれる通信傍受プログラム　**PRISM**「プリズム」NSA運営の情報収集プログラム。米中央情報局（CIA）元職員のエドワード・スノーデン（Edward Snowden）氏は、これがインターネット監視システムであると内部告発を行った。　**whistleblower**「内部告発者，公益通報者」企業・職場の不正を通報する人　**surefire**「絶対確実な，成功間違いなしの」　**infringe**「（権利を）侵害する」　**go a long way**「非常に役立つ，大きな役割を果たす」

QUESTIONS FOR UNDERSTANDING

Look at the following statements. Write T if the statement is True, and F if it is False. Write the number of the paragraph where you find the answer in the parenthesis.

1. _____ In 2013, identity theft was estimated to have cost over $100 billion.　　　　　　　　　　　　　　　　　　　　　　　　　　　　(#　　)

2. _____ Conficker is a very sophisticated worm that was created to send spam.　(#　　)

3. _____ The cyber-attack "Cuckoo's Nest" was carried out by North Korea in 1986.　(#　　)

4. _____ Edward Snowden has helped us to fully understand the extent of the PRISM program.　(#　　)

5. _____ It is still possible to protect ourselves from cyber-attacks and cyber spying.　(#　　)

Chapter 19 Someone Is Watching Me—Cyber-spies and Cyber-warfare

SUMMARY

Fill each space with the best word or phrase from the list below.

| acknowledge | illegal | criminals |
| devastating | intelligence services | cybercrime |

The Internet has brought with it great convenience and great risks. 1)_____ is now a global phenomenon costing over $100 billion per year, and the number of 2)_____ attacks on governments, organizations, and individuals is increasing all the time. Sometimes the cyber-attacks can be 3)_____, as with the Stuxnet worm. In other cases, such as with the Conficker worm, the aim of the 4)_____ seems to be the sending of spam. Whether it is the 5)_____ of a particular country or other organizations and individuals, the pace and ubiquity of cyber-attacks and cyber-spying is evident. Given the sophistication of the technology involved, we have to 6)_____ that it may become impossible to fully protect ourselves from cyber-attacks and cyber-spying in the future.

DATA ANALYSIS

Use the information in the passage to complete the following table.

Name of Virus/Worm/Cyber attack/Government program	Year	Target	Effect/Importance
Stuxnet			
	2008		
		An American military network	
			Ability to spy taken to a new level
PRISM			

CHAPTER 20
Everybody Wants to Rule the World
How Does International Law Work?

GETTING READY

Choose the correct word or phrase from the list below to complete the story.

1. The League of Nations is an example of an organization set up to promote _____.

2. It was set up after the First World War and one of its aims was to _____ the possibility of future wars.

3. The League did have some early successes such as when it resolved the _____ between Germany and Poland over Upper Silesia in 1921.

4. The organization started to break down in the 1930s as major powers withdrew and it became impossible to _____ peace in the build-up to the Second World War.

5. Although the League was ultimately unsuccessful, it did have a(n) _____ impact on international law in the 20th century because much of its framework was incorporated into the founding of the United Nations in 1945.

| international law | enormous | maintain | dispute | eliminate |

READING

On April 1, 2001, a United States Navy aircraft collided with a Chinese jet fighter over the South China Sea. The incident was 110 km from the Chinese island of Hainan and 160 km from a Chinese military installation. The Chinese authorities thought that the U.S. plane had been flying in its territory whereas the
5 U.S. authorities claimed that its plane had been flying in international waters — areas which do not belong to any country. The two countries' disagreement can be traced back to the United Nations Convention on the Law of the Sea. The Chinese

government, like most countries, had signed this agreement while the U.S. government had not. As a result, it was possible to say that both countries' claims were right or both were wrong.

2 The Hainan Island Incident is an example of a dispute in international law. International law is a set of rules that are accepted by states and nations. These rules are contained in numerous conventions, charters, and agreements. However, states are not necessarily required to abide by these laws. Rather, they agree to be bound by them only when their government ratifies them.

International law is difficult because it must balance the competing interests of different countries.

3 The United Nations (U.N.), formed in 1945 after the Second World War, has been heavily involved in the development of international law. Documents such as the U.N. Charter, The Universal Declaration of Human Rights, the Convention of the Rights of the Child, and the Statute of the International Court of Justice, are significant parts of modern international law. Chapter 1 of the U.N. Charter has four main aims: to maintain peace and international security, to develop friendly relations among nations, to achieve international co-operation in solving a variety of international problems, and to make the U.N. a center for harmonizing the actions of its members. The U.N. started with only 51 members, but its 193 members today include almost every country in the world except Kosovo, Taiwan, and The Vatican.

4 The U.N. has had some significant successes in peacekeeping, including action in Sierra Leone, Burundi, Côte d'Ivoire, Timor-Leste, Liberia, Haiti, and Kosovo, and it was awarded the Nobel Peace Prize in 1988. However, the U.N. does not always perform so well, and understanding why helps us to understand some of the difficulties involved in upholding international law.

5 The recent civil war in Syria is a good example. The U.N. Security Council tried to condemn the war four times, but each time one or more members vetoed U.N. action. The U.N. also tried to refer the matter to the International Criminal Court (ICC). However, Syria was not a member of the ICC, and so it was not bound by its rules. The truth is that any country, especially a powerful country, can ignore international law whenever it suits them, and they often do. A good example of this is Russia's annexation of Crimea, which violated a number of international laws. Unfortunately, if a powerful country decides to ignore international law, other countries have to decide whether they will take military action to right these wrongs. In most cases, national leaders are not willing to take such a major step.

6 International law should not be considered a failure, however. For example, the Geneva Conventions were created successively in 1864, 1906, and 1929, and updated in 1949. They define the rules that apply to armed conflict and the protection of the people not directly involved in fighting, such as sick and wounded soldiers. It also applies to the treatment of prisoners of war and the treatment of civilians. It may be argued that this set of international laws has saved thousands of lives and reduced the suffering of many more due to its existence. Other successful international laws have nearly eliminated the use of landmines (the 1997 Ottawa Treaty) and chemical and biological weapons (the 1997 Chemical Weapons Convention and the 1975 Biological Weapons Convention), and outlawed torture (the 1984 U.N. Convention Against Torture). International laws we may not even be aware of keep us safe by providing the rules for international shipping (controlled by the International Maritime Organization) and air travel (controlled by the International Civil Aviation Organization).

7 International law is a complex and unwieldy issue. There are many conventions, treaties, protocols, and agreements governing all areas of international activity. Despite the good intentions of those that frame these laws, they often appear to be ineffective as states often choose to ignore the rules or withdraw from agreements when it suits them. Despite these challenges, however, international law can be shown to have produced an enormous amount of good. It would seem that continuing efforts to improve and enforce international law serve a valuable purpose for the international community.

Chapter 20 Everybody Wants to Rule the World—How Does International Law Work?

NOTES

international law「国際法」　**League of Nations**「(the〜)国際連盟」1920年のベルサイユ条約にも基づいて結成され、1946年に現在の国際連合にその理念と枠組みが引き継がれた。　**Silesia**「シュレジエン」ヨーロッパ中東部オーデル川の上中流地域に広がる地方。もとは主にドイツ領で、現在大部分はポーランド領。　**build-up**「（緊張・交通量の）高まり」　**Hainan**「海南，海南島，海南省」中国・南シナ海上の島で、一省を成す。　**military installation**「軍事施設」　**international waters**「国際水域」どの国の領海・内水・群島水域でもない水域。公海。⇔ territorial waters　**United Nations Convention on the Law of the Sea**「(the〜)国連海洋法条約」略：UNCLOS　**U.N. Charter**「(the〜)国連憲章」　**Universal Declaration of Human Rights**「(the〜)世界人権宣言」　**Convention of the Rights of the Child**「(the〜)子どもの権利条約」　**Statute of the International Court of Justice**「(the〜)国際司法裁判所規定」　**veto**「拒否権を行使する，否認する」　**International Criminal Court (ICC)**「(the〜)国際刑事裁判所」集団殺戮の罪、人道に対する犯罪、戦争犯罪、侵略犯罪について、個人を国際法に基づき裁く。2002年にオランダのハーグに設立された。　**Russia's annexation of Crimea**「ロシアによるクリミア併合」クリミア半島は旧ソ連時代の1954年にロシアからウクライナに編入された歴史的経緯がある。2013年秋以降、EUとの統合を断念した親ロシア政権への反発が広がり、2014年2月に政権が崩壊、その後ロシア系住民の多いクリミアにロシア軍とみられる部隊が展開した。クリミア自治共和国では住民投票が行われ、ロシア編入への賛成票が95%を超え、議会がウクライナからの独立を宣言、2014年3月18日にロシアはクリミアを併合した。これに対し米欧は、軍事的脅威による領土略奪であると批判を強め、G8（主要8カ国）からロシアを排除した。　**Geneva Convention**「(the〜)ジュネーブ条約」戦時における傷病者と捕虜に関する国際条約。1864年に締結された赤十字条約に始まる。現在の条約は4条約と1977年の2つの議定書から成る。　**Ottawa Treaty**「オタワ条約」対人地雷全面禁止条約の通称。正式名称はThe Convention on the Prohibition of the Use, Stockpiling, Production and Transfer of Anti-Personnel Mines and on their Destruction「対人地雷の使用、貯蔵、生産及び移譲の禁止並びに廃棄に関する条約」　**Chemical Weapons Convention**「化学兵器禁止条約」略：CWC　正式名称はThe Convention on the Prohibition of the Development, Production, Stockpiling and Use of Chemical Weapons and on Their Destruction「化学兵器の開発、生産、貯蔵及び使用の禁止並びに廃棄に関する条約」。サリンなどの化学兵器の開発・生産・保有などを包括的に禁止し、同時に米ロなどが保有している化学兵器を一定期間内（原則として10年以内）に全廃することを定めたもの。　**Biological Weapons Convention**「生物兵器禁止条約」略：BWC　正式名称は「細菌兵器（生物兵器）及び毒素兵器の開発，生産及び貯蔵の禁止並びに廃棄に関する条約」。生物・毒素兵器を包括的に禁止する唯一の多国間の法的枠組み。化学兵器および生物兵器の戦時での使用を禁止したジュネーブ議定書（1925）を受け、生物兵器の開発・製造貯蔵等を禁止するとともに、すでに保有されている生物兵器を廃棄することを目的とする。　**U.N. Convention Against Torture**「拷問禁止条約」正式名称はThe Convention against Torture and Other Cruel, Inhuman or Degrading Treatment or Punishment「拷問及び他の残虐な、非人道的な又は品位を傷つける取り扱い又は、刑罰に関する条約」1984年の第39回国連総会において採択され、1987年に発効した。日本は1999年に加入。　**International Maritime Organization**「国際海事機関」略：IMO　1958年に正式に発足した国連の専門機関の1つ。海上交通の安全と海洋汚染防止のための各国間協力を進める。　**International Civil Aviation Organization**「国際民間航空機関」略：ICAO　1944年の国際民間航空条約に基づき、1947年に設立された国連の専門機関の1つ。

Questions for Understanding

Check the best answer for each question.

1. What did the Hainan Island incident demonstrate?
   a. ☐ That Chinese claims to the waters being in their territory were correct.
   b. ☐ That American claims to the waters being in international territory were correct.
   c. ☐ That the U.N. Convention of the Law of the Sea does not work very well.
   d. ☐ That the Chinese and American governments are looking to expand their territories.

2. Which of the following is *not* a core aim of the U.N.?
   a. ☐ Promoting international law conferences
   b. ☐ Encouraging better relations between countries
   c. ☐ Maintaining international peace
   d. ☐ Providing a forum for discussion between countries

3. According to the passage, why does the U.N. often fail to prevent breaches in international law?
   a. ☐ It does not have the resources to intervene in disputes.
   b. ☐ Members often disregard rules when those rules don't suit them.
   c. ☐ More powerful countries have not signed up to the U.N.
   d. ☐ Countries are generally more focused on their own domestic issues.

4. Why might the Geneva Conventions be regarded as a success?
   a. ☐ There have been very few wars in the last 50 years.
   b. ☐ They have saved many lives due to the reduction of landmines.
   c. ☐ They are becoming more widely observed by member states and therefore effective.
   d. ☐ They have reduced needless loss of life during armed conflicts.

Chapter 20 Everybody Wants to Rule the World—How Does International Law Work?

Summary

Fill each space with the best word from the list below.

| despite | treaty | enforce | intentions | landmines | violate |

International law in principle makes perfect sense. In practice, 1)_____ its good 2)_____, it is often not effective. Recent disputes in Syria and Crimea have shown how hard it is to 3)_____ international law at times. When countries 4)_____ international law, it is hard to get different countries to agree on a course of action to fix the problem. Additionally, when military assistance is needed, many countries just don't want to risk their own soldiers in some far-off land. We should not forget about the successes of international law, though. The Ottawa 5)_____, for example, has helped to dramatically reduce the number of 6)_____ around the world, and there have also been successful steps to outlaw chemical and biological weapons. We should not disregard these achievements and recognize that international law, in spite of various challenges, has brought a lot of good to the world.

References

Compiled References

Many references were consulted in writing this book. The following is a list of the most useful, and we direct students and teachers who are interested in learning more about the issues raised in this book to them.

Books

Dalby, A, (2002). *Dangerous Tastes: The Story of Spices*, University of California Press, Oakland.

Ferguson, N. (2008). *The Ascent of Money: A Financial History of the World*, Allen Lane, London.

Lehrer, J. (2009) *How We Decide*, Houghton Mifflin Harcourt, New York.

Opie I. and Opie, P. (1997). *The Oxford Dictionary of Nursery Rhymes* (2nd ed), Oxford University Press, Oxford.

Willard, P. (2002). *Secrets of Saffron: The Vagabond Life of the World's Most Seductive Spice*, Beacon Press, Boston.

Papers

Boergers, J., Gable, C.J., Owens, J.A. (2014). Later School Start Time Is Associated with Improved Sleep and Daytime Functioning in Adolescents. *Journal of Behavioral Developmental Pediatrics, 35*(1), pp. 11-17.

Boland, T., Mironov, V., Gulowska, A., Roth, E.A., Markwald, R.R. (2003). Cell and organ printing 2: Fusion of cell aggregates in three-dimensional gels. *The Anatomical Record, 272A*(2), pp. 497–502.

Ciarleglio, C.M., Axley, J.C., Strauss, B.R., Gamble, K.L., McMahon, D.G. (2011). Perinatal photoperiod imprints the circadian clock. *Nature Neuroscience, 14*, pp. 25–27.

Disanto, G., Handel, A.E., Para, A.E., Ramagopalan, S. V., Handunnetthi, L. (2011). Season of birth and anorexia nervosa. *The British Journal of Psychiatry, 198*, pp. 404-405.

Herzer, D. and Vollmer, S. (2013). Rising top incomes do not raise the tide. *Journal of Policy Modeling, 35*(4), pp. 504-519.

Honda, G. (1997). "Differential Structure, Differential Health: Industrialization in Japan, 1868-1940" in Steckel, R.H. and Floud, R. (eds), *Health and Welfare during Industrialization*, University of Chicago Press, Chicago, pp.251-284.

Kripke, D.F., Garfinkel, L., Wingard, D.L, Klauber, M.R, Marler, M.R (2002). Mortality Associated With Sleep Duration and Insomnia. *Archives of*

General Psychiatry, 59(2), pp.131-136.

Low, P.S., Shank, S.S., Sejnowski, T.J., Margoliash, D. (2008). Mammalian-like features of sleep structure in zebra finches. *PNAS, 105*(26), pp. 9081-9086.

Mattila, A.S., and Wirtz, J. (2001). Congruency of scent and music as a driver of in-store evaluations and behavior. *Journal of Retailing, 77*, pp. 273–289.

Murphy, S.V. and Atala, A. (2014). 3D bioprinting of tissues and organs. *Nature Biotechnology, 32*, pp 773–785.

Mironov, V., Boland, T., Trusk, T., Forgacs, G., Markwald, R.R. (2003). Organ printing: computer-aided jet-based 3D tissue engineering. *Trends in Biotechnology, 21*(4), pp 157–161.

Woods, J., Williams, A., Hughes, J.K., Black, M., Murphy, R. (2010). Energy and the food system. Philosophical Transactions of the Royal Society B, *365*(1554), pp 2991-3006.

Yoneshiro, T., Aita, S., Kawai, Y., Iwanaga, T., Saito, M. (2012). Nonpungent capsaicin analogs (capsinoids) increase energy expenditure through the activation of brown adipose tissue in humans, *American Journal of Clinical Nutrition, 95*, pp. 845–850.

Reports

Bebchuk, L and Grinstein, Y. (2005). *The Growth of Executive Pay,* Harvard Law School, 2005.

Bradbear, N., "Bees and their role in forest livelihoods. A guide to the services provided by bees and the sustainable harvesting, processing and marketing of their products." In *Non-Wood Forest Products (FAO), no. 19*, Food and Agriculture Organization of the United Nations (FAO), Forest Products and Industries Division, 2009.

Harvest Consulting Group, *BrandSense: Building Brands with Sensory Experiences*, Harvest Consulting Group, 2001.

Frydman, C. (2008). *Learning from the Past: Trends in Executive Compensation over the Twentieth Century*, CESIFO Working Paper no. 2460, CESIFO, 2008.

Hanboonsong, Y., Jamjanya, T., Durst, P.B. *Six-legged livestock: edible insect farming, collection on and marketing in Thailand,* Food and Agriculture Organization of the United Nations (FAO), Regional Office for Asia and the Pacific, 2013.

Heinrich Böll Foundation, *Meat Atlas: Facts and figures about the animals we eat*, Heinrich Böll Foundation and Friends of the Earth Europe, 2014.

Huis, A., Itterbeeck, J.A., Klunder, H., Mertens, E., Halloran, A., Muir, G., Vantomme, P. *Edible insects: future prospects for food and feed security,*

FAO Forestry Paper, no. 171, Food and Agriculture Organization of the United Nations (FAO), Forest Products and Industries Division, 2013.

Kentucky Cooperative Extension Service, *Beekeeping and Honey Production*, University of Kentucky, College of Agriculture, 2013.

Market and Policy Analyses of Raw Materials, Horticulture and Tropical (RAMHOT) Products Team. *Banana Market Review and Banana Statistics 2012-2013*, Food and Agriculture Organization of the United Nations (FAO), Rome, 2014.

OECD (2014). *Focus on Inequality and Growth – December 2014*, Directorate for Employment, Labour and Social Affairs, OECD, 2014.

Symantec Corporation, *International Security Threat Report 2014, Volume 19*, Symantec Corporation, 2014.

The Economist Intelligence Unit, *Global food security index 2014*, The Economist Intelligence Unit, 2014.

USAID, *World Market for Honey*, Capacity to Improve Agriculture and Food Security, USAID, 2012.

Walk Free Foundation, *Global Slavery Index 2013*, Walk Free Foundation, 2013.

Articles

"An appalling waste of food," *The Japan Times*, 21 January 2013.

Carey, S. "Airlines Try Signature Fragrances, but Not Everyone Is On Board," *The Wall Street Journal*, 1 February 2015.

Coghlan, A., "Fat lab lock-in: Can spicy pills help you lose weight?" *New Scientist*, no. 2875 (July 2012).

Dorling, D., "How the super rich got richer: 10 shocking facts about inequality," *The Guardian*, 15 September 2014.

Dominiczak, P. "Cyber spies join forces to keep Britain and US safe from web terrorists," *The Telegraph*, 18 January 2015.

Gellman, B. "NSA broke privacy rules thousands of times per year, audit finds," *The Washington Post*, 15 August 2013.

Grossman, L. and Marks, P., "Space-miners to crush asteroids and 3D print satellites," *New Scientist*, no. 2901 (January 2013).

Harney, A. and Slodkowski, A. "Interns abused as labor crisis grows," *The Japan Times*, 13 June 2014.

Hodson, H., "The personal nudge," *New Scientist*, no. 2942 (November 2013).

"Inequality: Inherited Wealth," *The Economist*, 18 March 2014.

"Hype and fear," *The Economist*, 8 December 2012.

MacKenzie, D., "Cinnamon spice produces healthier blood" *New Scientist*, no. 2422 (November 2003).

Marks, P., "Who owns asteroids or the moon?" *New Scientist*, no. 2867 (June 2012).

Marks, P. and MacGregor, C., "Water central to detailed asteroid mining mission plan," *New Scientist*, no. 2862 (April 2012).

Marks, P., "Vertical farms sprouting all over the world," *New Scientist*, no. 2952 (January 2014).

Pearce, F., "Going bananas," *New Scientist*, no. 2378 (January 2003).

Pearce, F., "To green the deserts, just add... seawater," *New Scientist*, no. 2918 (May 2013).

"Recycling machine turns plastic bottles into food for stray dogs," *The Telegraph*, 24 July 2014.

Ronald, P., "Future farms need to use every trick in the book," *New Scientist*, no. 2886 (October 2012).

Rutkin, A., "Books out, 3D printers in for reinvented US libraries," *New Scientist*, no. 2978 (July 2014).

Rutkin, A. "Off the Clock, On the Record," *New Scientist*, no.2991 (October 2014).

Spence P., "20th Anniversary of First Online Sale: How We Shop on the Web," *The Telegraph*, 11 August 2014.

Takada, A. "Farmers fattening pigs with recycled food," *The Japan Times*, 5 July 2014.

Thau, B., "New Study Reveals Why Consumers Really Shop Online (Surprise: It Isn't Low Prices)," *Forbes*, 10 August 2013

Tucker, A. "Jellyfish: The Next King of the Sea," *Smithsonian Magazine* (August 2010).

"Turning worm," *The Economist,* 13 December 2014.

Walker, S. "Russia celebrates anniversary of Crimea takeover – and eyes second annexation," *The Guardian,* 18 March 2015.

"World Gourmet Cuisine," *Public Affairs Department Singapore Airlines Ltd* (June 2011).

Broadcasts

Can Eating Insects Save the World?, Kari Lia (Director), British Broadcasting Corporation, UK, 24 June 2014.

Koller, D. (June 2012). *What we're learning from online education*, [Video file]. Retrieved from <http://www.ted.com/talks/daphne_koller_what_we_re_learning_from_online_education?language=en#t-1129959> (accessed 10 March, 2015).

Webpages

Alford, J. "3D Printed Body Parts Go Mainstream," *IFLScience!*, 19 May 2014, <http://www.iflscience.com/technology/3d-printed-body-parts-go-mainstream> (accessed 21 September 2014).

Alford, J. "Doctors Use 3D-Printed Replica Brains To Guide Life-Changing Pediatric Surgery," *IFLScience!*, 10 September 2014, <http://www.iflscience.com/health-and-medicine/doctors-use-3d-printed-replica-brains-guide-life-changing-pediatric-surgery> (accessed 21 September 2014).

Alford, J. "Using 3D Printers To Generate Villages Of Houses," *IFLScience!*, 17 April 2014, <http://www.iflscience.com/technology/using-3d-printers-generate-villages-houses> (accessed 21 September 2014).

Alternative Fuels Data Center "Electric Vehicle Charging Station Locations" <http://www.afdc.energy.gov/fuels/electricity_locations.html> (accessed 23 March 2015).

"Artificial blood vessels created on a 3D printer," *BBC News Online*, 16 September 2011, <http://www.bbc.co.uk/news/technology-14946808> (accessed 21 October 2011).

Ball, J., Borger, J. and Greenwald, G. "Revealed: how US and UK spy agencies defeat internet privacy and security," *The Guardian,* 6 September 2013, <http://www.theguardian.com/world/2013/sep/05/nsa-gchq-encryption-codes-security> (accessed 10 February 2015).

"Banana facts and figures" *Food and Agriculture Organization of the United Nations (FAO)* <http://www.fao.org/economic/est/est-commodities/bananas/bananafacts/en/#.VCjaRlf4UjE> (accessed 29 September 2014).

"Best In-Flight Dining," *Saveur.com,* <http://www.saveur.com/content/culinary-travel-awards-2014-winners-best-in-flight-dining-economy-class> (accessed 9 June 2014).

Booton, J., "Alibaba's 'Singles Day' sales top $9 billion, bigger than Black Friday," *Marketwatch,* 11 November 2014

<http://www.marketwatch.com/story/alibabas-singles-day-bigger-than-black-friday-2014-11-10> (accessed 6 April 2015)

Bummel, A. "The failure of the UN: rebuilding from the ruins," *openSecurity*, 1 September 2014, <https://www.opendemocracy.net/opensecurity/andreas-bummel/failure-of-un-rebuilding-from-ruins> (accessed 19 March 2015).

"Bungling banana robber is jailed," *BBC News Online*, 16 March 2005, <http://news.bbc.co.uk/1/hi/england/london/4354919.stm> (accessed 27 February 2015).

"Did the Forbes 400 Billionaires Really 'Build That'?" *CNBC*, 25 September 2012, <http://www.cnbc.com/id/49167533> (accessed 12 June 2014).

"Electric Eel Shock", *Wikipedia.org* <http://en.wikipedia.org/wiki/Electric_Eel_Shock> (accessed 17 March 2015).

Ferro, S. "Check This Out: A 3-D Printer Made From E-Waste," *Popular Science*, 10 October 2013, <http://www.popsci.com/article/diy/check-out-3-d-printer-made-e-waste> (accessed 21 May 2014).

"'Follow the Money': NSA Spies on International Payments," *Spiegel Online International*, 15 September 2013, <http://www.spiegel.de/international/world/spiegel-exclusive-nsa-spies-on-international-bank-transactions-a-922276.html> (accessed 19 May 2014).

Food and Agriculture Organization of the United Nations (FAO), FAOSTAT online statistical service <http://faostat.fao.org/> (accessed March 10, 2012).

Genthon, P. "Blue and green honey makes French beekeepers see red," *Reuters*, 5 October 2012 <http://www.reuters.com/article/2012/10/05/us-france-bees-idUSBRE8930MQ20121005> (accessed 26 September 2014).

Greenberg, A. "How 3-D Printed Guns Evolved Into Serious Weapons in Just One Year," *Wired.com*, 15 May 2014, <http://www.wired.com/2014/05/3d-printed-guns/> (accessed 21 September 2014).

"Hainan Island Incident," *Wikipedia.org*, <http://en.wikipedia.org/wiki/Hainan_Island_incident> (accessed 19 March 2015).

"How 3D printing is changing the shape of lessons," *BBC News Online*, 15 April 2014, <http://www.bbc.com/news/business-26871084> (accessed 21 May 2014).

"How online retail has changed the way we shop," *BBC News Online*, 11 August 2014,

<http://www.bbc.com/news/business-28739570> (accessed 6 April 2015).

Hubbard, K. "When should you toss out food?" *BBC News Online*, 24 September 2014, <http://www.bbc.com/capital/story/20140923-dont-toss-out-that-food-yet> (accessed 26 September 2014).

"International Law," *Wikipedia.org*, <http://en.wikipedia.org/wiki/International_law> (accessed 19 March 2015).

"Japan man held over '3D-printed guns'," *BBC News Online*, 8 May 2014, <http://www.bbc.com/news/technology-27322947> (accessed 21 May 2014).

Kraft, R., McMahan, T., and Henry, K. "NASA Tests Limits of 3-D Printing with Powerful Rocket Engine Check," *NASA Press Release 13-260*, 27 August 2013, <http://www.nasa.gov/press/2013/august/nasa-tests-limits-of-3-d-printing-with-powerful-rocket-engine-check/> (accessed 21 September 2013).

Kraft, R., McMahan, T., and Henry, K. "NASA Tests Limits of 3-D Printing with Powerful Rocket Engine Check," *NASA*, 27 August 2013, <http://www.nasa.gov/press/2013/august/nasa-tests-limits-of-3-d-printing-with-powerful-rocket-engine-check/> (accessed 21 September 2013).

"List of Nobel Peace Prize laureates," *Wikipedia.org*, <http://en.wikipedia.org/wiki/List_of_Nobel_Peace_Prize_laureates> (accessed 19 March 2015).

"Make-It-Yourself: The rise of the micro-manufacturers," *BBC News Online*, 23 September 2013, <http://www.bbc.com/news/business-24203938> (accessed 21 May 2014).

McCarthy, E. "13 Products Made Using Recycled Materials," *mental_floss.com* <http://mentalfloss.com/article/50227/13-products-made-using-recycled-materials> (accessed 17 August 2014).

Murtagh, J. "Successful marketing demands use of all five senses," *The Dreamspeaker,* <http://www.thedreamspeaker.com/successful-marketing-demands-use-of-all-five-senses/> (accessed 12 March 2015).

NASA. "3D Printer Headed to Space Station," *NASA*, 18 September 2014, <http://www.nasa.gov/content/3d-printer-headed-to-space-station//> (accessed 21 September 2014).

Norris, A. "Wearable technology: 2015 is the year of the smart bra," *The Telegraph*, 27December 2014, <http://www.telegraph.co.uk/news/predictions/technology/11306735/wearable-technology-trend.html> (accessed 26 March 2015).

"New global index exposes 'modern slavery' worldwide," *BBC News Online*, 17 October 2013, <http://www.bbc.co.uk/news/world-24560937> (accessed 21 October 2013).

Ramaswamy, S., "Shopping Then and Now: Five Ways Retail Has Changed and How Businesses Can Adapt," *www.thinkwithgoogle.com* <www.thinkwithgoogle.com/articles/five-ways-retail-has-changed-and-how-businesses-can-adapt.html> (accessed 6 April 2015).

"Recycled Paradise: Amazing Man-Made Floating Island," *doorknob.com* <http://dornob.com/recycled-paradise-amazing-man-made-floating-island/> (accessed 26 February 2015).

"Recycling Guide," *Guides Network* <http://www.recycling-guide.org.uk/reduce.html> (accessed 25 January 2015).

"Richard Axel and Linda Buck Awarded 2004 Nobel Prize in Physiology or Medicine," *Howard Hughes Medical Institute,* 4 October 2004 <http://

www.hhmi.org/news/richard-axel-and-linda-buck-awarded-2004-nobel-prize-physiology-or-medicine> (accessed 11 April 2014).

Schaal, E. "The 10 Electric Vehicles With the Longest Driving Range" 16 January 2015

<http://www.cheatsheet.com/automobiles/top-10-electric-vehicles-with-the-longest-driving-range.html/?a=viewall#ixzz3VAZwmMKY> (accessed 23 March 2015).

Shadbolt, P. "Hong Kong's fish farms in the sky," *BBC News Online*, 2 April 2014, <http://www.bbc.com/news/business-26627408> (accessed 21 September 2014).

"Spiral Island," *Wikipedia.org*, <http://en.wikipedia.org/wiki/Spiral_Island> (accessed 10 January 2015).

Smialek, J. "The 1% May Be Richer Than You Think, Research Shows," *Bloomberg*, 7 August 2014, <http://www.bloomberg.com/news/2014-08-06/the-1-may-be-richer-than-you-think-research-shows.html> (accessed 10 August 2014).

"The 2013 Legatum Prosperity Index" *Legatum Institute* <http://www.prosperity.com/> (accessed 10 August 2014).

"The companies vying to turn asteroids into filling stations," *BBC News Online*, 25 September 2014, <http://www.bbc.com/news/magazine-29334645> (accessed 25 September 2014).

"The Poor Little Rich Girl," *Wikipedia.org*, <http://en.wikipedia.org/wiki/The_Poor_Little_Rich_Girl> (accessed 10 August 2014).

"The rise of click and collect for online shoppers," *BBC News Online*, 2 May 2014,

<http://www.bbc.com/news/business-27251111> (accessed 6 April 2015).

"The world's most visited countries - 2014," *Telegraph Travel,* <http://www.telegraph.co.uk/travel/travelnews/11027765/The-worlds-most-visited-countries-2014.html> (accessed 13 January 2015).

"Uphold International Law," *United Nations,* < http://www.un.org/en/sections/what-we-do/uphold-international-law/index.html> (accessed 19 March 2015).

"What kinds of products are made from recycled PET?," *CPME,* 3 March 2011, <http://www.cpme-pet.org/content/what-kinds-products-are-made-recycled-pet> (accessed 10 March 2015).

"Where are you on the global pay scale?" *BBC News Online*, 29 March 2012, <http://www.bbc.com/news/magazine-17512040> (accessed 21 May 2014).

Winter, L. "Empty Electronics Factories Turned Into High-Tech Indoor Farms," *IFLScience!*, 11 July 2014, <http://www.iflscience.com/technology/empty-electronics-factories-turned-high-tech-indoor-farms> (accessed 21

September 2014).

Winter, L. "Made-To-Order Cartilage Could Combat Osteoarthritis," *IFLScience!*, 28 April 2014, <http://www.iflscience.com/health-and-medicine/made-order-cartilage-could-combat-osteoarthritis> (accessed 21 September 2014).

Winter, L. "Man Constructs 3D Printed Concrete Castle," *IFLScience!*, 4 September 2014, <http://www.iflscience.com/technology/man-constructs-3d-printed-concrete-castle> (accessed 21 September 2014).

Vance, A. "The Cult of Elon Musk: A Night With the 'D' and Thousands of Tesla Fanatics" 10 October 2104, <http://www.bloomberg.com/bw/articles/2014-10-10/tesla-debuts-the-d-a-night-in-la-with-the-cult-of-elon-musk> (accessed 23 March 2015).

Zobel, G, "Alfredo Moser: Bottle light inventor proud to be poor," *BBC News Online*, 13 August 2013, <http://www.bbc.com/news/magazine-23536914> (accessed 17 December 2014).

Websites

https://www.kickstarter.com/?ref=nav

http://www.gofundme.com/?pc=cf2

http://landing.indiegogo.com/indiegogo-basics

https://www.coursera.org/

http://online-learning.harvard.edu/

https://www.coursera.org/

http://www.jmooc.jp/?lang=ja

https://www.edx.org/

https://www.futurelearn.com/

https://www.udemy.com/

http://www.google.com/glass/start/

http://www.fitbit.com/jp#i.qj5nyv5u9di0s1

https://www.apple.com/watch/

http://www.pilot-b2p.eu/b2p-pens

http://www.lowcarbon.co.uk/

TEXT PRODUCTION STAFF

edited by Kimio Sato	編集 佐藤 公雄
English-language editing by Bill Benfield	英文校閲 ビル・ベンフィールド
cover design by Ruben Frosali	表紙デザイン ルーベン・フロサリ
text design by Ruben Frosali	本文デザイン ルーベン・フロサリ

CD PRODUCTION STAFF

narrated by Lindsay Rebecca Nelson (AmE) Bill Sullivan (AmE)	吹き込み者 リンジー・レベッカ・ネルソン（アメリカ英語） ビル・サリバン（アメリカ英語）

World of Wonders Inspiring the Future
知の挑戦

2016年1月20日　初版発行
2019年2月25日　第6刷発行

編著者　　Anthony Sellick
　　　　　John Barton
　　　　　小笠原 亜衣

発行者　　佐野 英一郎

発行所　　株式会社 成美堂
　　　　　〒101-0052　東京都千代田区神田小川町3-22
　　　　　TEL 03-3291-2261　FAX 03-3293-5490
　　　　　https://www.seibido.co.jp

印刷・製本　倉敷印刷（株）

ISBN 978-4-7919-4796-6　　　　　　　　　　　Printed in Japan

・落丁・乱丁本はお取り替えします。
・本書の無断複写は、著作権上の例外を除き著作権侵害となります。

MEMO

MEMO

MEMO